C000233702

The Rou
of Lamb....

Politics, Property and Peculation
in Victorian London

A History of William Roupell
M.P. for Lambeth 1857 - 1862

by
Judy Harris

The Streatham Society

First published in 2001 for

The Streatham Society
219 Sternhold Avenue
Streatham
London SW2 4PG

by

Local History Publications
316 Green Lane
Streatham
London SW16 3AS

ISBN 1 873520 37 9

CONTENTS

LIST OF ILLUSTRATIONS

4

ACKNOWLEDGEMENTS

Grateful thanks for the help and encouragement given by the following: in particular, Jim Cox, whose idea it was, and Brian Bloice, without whom it would have neither been started nor finished. In preparing the text for publication, I am indebted to John Brown, David Hayter and Charles Watson for their considerable help and advice.

Also:

Members of the Streatham Society Local History Group, particularly John Brown, John Cresswell, Graham Gower, Keith Holdaway and Bob Jenner

Members of the Southwark and Lambeth Archaeological Society, particularly Roy Edwards, Graham Gibberd and George Young

Jane Baker

Robin Brand and the research of CW Brand

Mrs D Lucy and Mrs Payne

Lt. Col. PG Roupell

The staff of Lambeth, Southwark and Wandsworth Archives

Other sources used:

In London:
British Library and Newspaper Library
Family Records Centre
Guildhall Library
Hyde Park Family History Centre at the Church of the Latter Day Saints
London Metropolitan Archives
Public Record Office
Society of Genealogists

Also:
Archives and Record Offices of Essex, Hampshire and Surrey
Harvard Law Library, USA

William Roupell as depicted in the Illustrated Weekly News of 4th October 1862

THE ROUPELLS OF LAMBETH

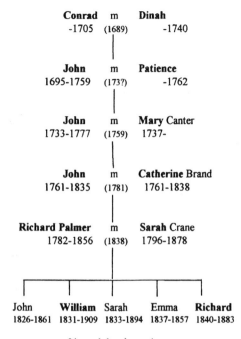

Conrad -1705	m (1689)	**Dinah** -1740	Captain in William III Guard Lived Strutton Ground, Westminster 6 children baptised Savoy Chapel Dinah buried St Andrew's, Holborn
John 1695-1759	m (173?)	**Patience** -1762	Jeweller in Dolphin Court, Ludgate Hill Lived Bangor Court, Shoe Lane 4 children baptised St Andrew's, Holborn Buried St Martin's, Ludgate
John 1733-1777	m (1759)	**Mary** Canter 1737-	Lived Shoe Lane and Stonecutter Street 4 children baptised St Martin's & St Andrew's John buried St Bride's, Fleet Street
John 1761-1835	m (1781)	**Catherine** Brand 1761-1838	Lead smelter, Bear Lane Lived Cross (Meymott) Street 1 child baptised St Bride's Buried St John's, Waterloo
Richard Palmer 1782-1856	m (1838)	**Sarah** Crane 1796-1878	Iron smelter, land owner, property developer Lived Cross Street and Roupell Park Five children Buried West Norwood cemetery

John	**William**	Sarah	Emma	**Richard**
1826-1861	1831-1909	1833-1894	1837-1857	1840-1883

Line ended, no known issue

Signature of John Roupell (1761-1835)

Signature of Richard Palmer Roupell (1782-1856)

Signature of Sarah Roupell (1796-1878)

Signature of William Roupell (1831-1909)

THE ROUPELL FAMILY CONNECTIONS

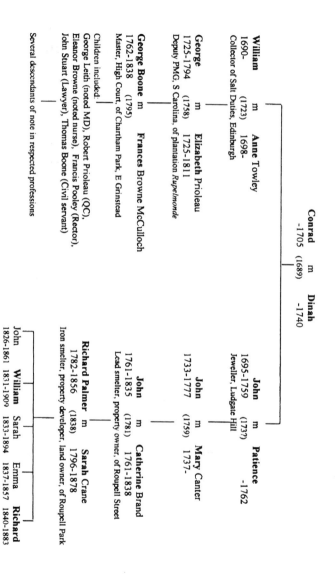

Conrad m (1689) **Dinah**
-1705   -1740

William m (1723) **Anne** Towley
1690-   1698-
Collector of Salt Duties, Edinburgh

George m (1758) **Elizabeth** Prioleau
1725-1794   1725-1811
Deputy PMG, S Carolina, of plantation *Rupelmonde*

George Boone m (1795) **Frances** Browne McCulloch
1762-1838
Master, High Court, of Chartham Park, E Grinstead

Children included:
George Leith (noted MD), Robert Prioleau (QC),
Eleanor Browne (noted nurse), Francis Pooley (Rector),
John Stuart (Lawyer), Thomas Boone (Civil servant)

Several descendants of note in respected professions

John m (1737?) **Patience**
1695-1759   -1762
Jeweller, Ludgate Hill

John m (1759) **Mary** Canter
1733-1777   1737-

John m (1781) **Catherine** Brand
1761-1835   1761-1838
Lead smelter, property owner, of Roupell Street

Richard Palmer m (1838) **Sarah** Crane
1782-1856   1796-1878
Iron smelter, property developer, land owner, of Roupell Park

John   **William**   Sarah   Emma   **Richard**
1826-1861   1831-1909   1833-1894   1837-1857   1840-1883

Line ended, no known issue

8

THE ROUPELLS OF LAMBETH

Introduction

On September 24th 1862, William Roupell, aged thirty-one, MP for Lambeth, was convicted of forgery at the Old Bailey and sentenced to penal servitude for life. This effectively ended the progress of one of South London's wealthy property-owning families. In less than ten years William had apparently spent over £200,000 and lost most of the land and property it had taken his father and grandfather fifty years to acquire. At present day values, this is a loss of a family fortune of over £8 million.

The Roupell wealth came from the family lead-smelting or, perhaps more accurately, scrap-metal business based at their factory in Bear Lane, Southwark. John and Richard Palmer Roupell, William's grandfather and father, lived in Cross Street, Blackfriars (now Meymott Street SE1). By the 1820s they owned various properties in the area, including the land which was to become Roupell Street.

In 1810, for some £3,000, the Roupells made their first major land purchase from the late Lord Thurlow's estate on Brixton Hill. Between 1810 and 1819 they paid a total of about £12,000 for this prime meadow and woodland hill site which was developed between 1840 and 1860 into the prestigious residential area of Roupell Park, surrounding Christchurch and Palace Roads, Streatham Hill SW2. The Roupells' speculative buying of farm land for future development was replicated in other areas in Surrey, Essex and Hampshire; but Roupell Park remained their most successful venture.

It was here on his country estate in 1839 that Richard Palmer Roupell built Aspen House on Brixton Hill for his wife and young family. But the wealthy Roupells hid a secret. It was only months previously that Richard Palmer Roupell and his wife Sarah had married. According to evidence given later at William's trial, Richard Palmer had always lived in dread of his father and did not own to Sarah's existence because, she being the daughter of a carpenter, the marriage would have met with disapproval and he would not have been left any property. Sarah Crane, known as Mrs Carter, lived in Pitt Street, Peckham (now East Surrey Grove), where Richard Palmer visited her each week on Sunday, returning to his parents' house in Cross Street on Monday morning. By 1837, Sarah had borne him four children: John, William, Sarah and Emma.

On December 6th 1838, three years after the death of his father John and nine days after proving his mother's will, of which he was the sole beneficiary, he married Sarah Crane in St Giles's Church, Camberwell. After his family's removal to their new home, Richard Palmer continued to live in the small house in Cross Street, but now he spent an extra day at Aspen House, visiting from Saturday afternoon to Monday morning. Their only legitimate child, Richard, was born in 1840.

Aspen House, Brixton Hill (c. 1905).

By 1853, their second son William was twenty-two, had been articled to an attorney, and was very much involved in the family business. His major interest lay in the development of the Roupell Park estate. He was dominated by his father who, while recognising his son's business acumen, was always careful to see his money was not squandered and made him an allowance of only £1 a week. William later complained that this had been insufficient for the lifestyle of the son of a prominent local family. He was soon heavily in debt to his uncle Watts, also an attorney and married to his mother's sister. In 1850, without his father's knowledge, he raised a loan using the Norbiton Park Farm estate in Surrey as security. In 1853, on his own admission, his first forgery was effected. A letter, supposedly from his father, gave him the Roupell Park estate. Over the next three years, with little apparent difficulty, William fraudulently obtained, then mortgaged, much of his father's property.

On September 12th 1856, Richard Palmer Roupell died at Cross Street. Finding his will in a strong box by his father's death bed, William discovered that the three main estates at Kingston, Great Warley and Roupell Park had all been left to sixteen-year-old Richard, the legitimate heir. William destroyed the will and forged another, dated ten days previously, leaving everything to his mother with himself as executor. Subsequently it was easy for him to obtain his mother's consent to the mortgaging or sale of most of the property.

William Roupell, convicted forger and ex-MP for Lambeth

In 1857 William Roupell, a land-owner, member of Lambeth Vestry and regarded as a local young man of great expectations, decided to stand for Parliament. After a campaign costing him in excess of £6,000, he received an unprecedented 9,318 votes and became one of two Liberal MPs for Lambeth. A petition set up to question his dubious electioneering methods was dismissed as 'frivolous and vexatious'.

In 1860 William became a founder member and Major-Commandant of the 19th Corps of the Surrey Rifles Volunteers, although he had no military experience. Much of the success of the Corps was owed to his enthusiastic leadership - and money. He spent considerable sums providing uniforms, weapons and a drill area for his troops.

Early in 1862 the good life ended after John Treadwell of Leigham Court, Streatham Hill, pressed for payment for land leased to Roupell. In March Roupell made an abortive attempt to raise more money. His mortgagees threatened foreclosure and, after burning a number of forged documents in his rooms at the Surrey Rifles' headquarters in Kennington, he absconded to Spain. He returned a few months later after a visit from his younger brother Richard. He attended Richmond Parish Church the following Sunday and was arrested in Kingston the next day to stand trial on his own admission of fraud and forgery.

Roupell & Others v Waite opened in Guildford on 16th August 1862, attracting considerable public interest. Richard, the legal heir, attempted to gain possession of Norbiton Park Farm from a Mr Waite, to whom William had conveyed it the previous year. The case alleging the forgery of his father's will was proved and William was sentenced at the Old Bailey to penal servitude for life. However, because of other trials pending, he avoided transportation. At Chelmsford the following year he faced a similar trial concerning an Essex estate, but the jury failed to reach a verdict and the case was dismissed.

He was released in 1876, after fourteen years' imprisonment spent mainly in Portland prison, Dorset. He returned to Aspen House, Roupell Park, to live with his mother and sister Sarah. He was present at the death of his mother, aged 81, two years later. She had less than £1,500 to leave to her daughter Sarah. Aspen House was sold to William Yeats Baker, iron master, art connoisseur and maternal grandfather of the writer Dennis Wheatley.

On his brother William's return to the area, Richard Roupell removed to Trunk Farm, Farnborough, Hampshire, one of his late father's properties still intact. He had spent almost ten years involved in litigation attempting to regain the family fortune, but with only limited success. After their mother's death in 1878, Sarah and William moved to a smaller house in Christchurch Road within sight of their former home. Richard died in 1883, aged forty-two. Sarah died in 1894, aged sixty.

William, the last of the Roupells, lived on until 1909. His sister Sarah had left him all her money: £126 14s 11d. In addition, he had been left an allowance of £1 a week by his brother Richard, significantly the amount which William had stated at his trial had been an inadequate allowance thirty-three years earlier.

After his sister's death, William moved to the adjacent Garden Lane, Christchurch Road, to a small gardener's cottage which he named Harvey Lodge. He was cared for to the end of his life by Ellen Wood and her husband Arthur, a gardener. William variously described himself in his later years as a retired barrister, an estate agent, a surveyor and a horticultural adviser. He tended a friend's nursery garden, was secretary of the Brixton, Streatham and Clapham Horticultural Society, which he had founded in 1860, and was very much involved with Christ Church and its associated organisations. Rather ironically, he was secretary of the Christ Church Slate Club!

He died in poverty at the age of seventy-seven. Over three hundred people attended his funeral service at Christ Church, which was filled with flowers, perhaps showing that his need for public acclaim had been to some degree realised. He was again a respected local figure who, it was considered, had atoned for his misdeeds. He was buried in the family vault in West Norwood Cemetery. The square stone slab, enclosed by four yew trees, can be seen at the top of the hill, from where the blocks of flats now covering the once grand Roupell Park are clearly visible.

But the Roupell story, although it ended with the death of William, did not start with him. In 1862 at his trial, when William Roupell faced bankruptcy and ruin, he told how his first debt had occurred because of his inadequate allowance and the inability of a friend to repay him a loan. William could not have known that one hundred and thirty-six years earlier his great-great-great grandmother Dinah faced similar charges and gave similar reasons.

THE FIRST HUNDRED YEARS

From Westminster to Lambeth
1689 - 1796

On 5th November 1688 William, Prince of Orange, landed at Brixham in Devon and, in a Dutch invasion welcomed by English Protestants, travelled to London to claim the British throne. His army included German mercenaries who had a long tradition of hiring themselves to foreign armies. Conrad Roupell (variously spelt Roepel and Rupel) was one of these, attaining the position of Captain in William III's Guard. He is recorded as being a native of Hesse-Cassel in Germany where the family appear to have been of local importance. A common family name in this part of northern Europe, it is preserved today in the place name Rupelmonde on the River Rupel, south-west of Antwerp in Belgium, presumably denoting their origins.

On 13th February 1689 William of Orange and his wife Mary were invited by Parliament to become King and Queen: William III and Mary II. They were cousins, nephew and niece of Charles II; William being the son of Charles's sister Mary and William II, Prince of Orange, and Mary the daughter of Charles's brother James II. They were crowned on 11th April 1689. Mary died in 1694 and William in 1702, when he was succeeded by Mary's sister Anne, until her death in 1714 ended the troubled reign of the House of Stuart and introduced the House of Hanover.

Conrad Roupell married Dinah in 1689. She appears to have been from a well-connected Dutch family and was probably part of the Royal Household. On 26th August 1689 Conrad was granted a pension of £40 per annum by warrant of King William and Queen Mary for his long and faithful service to them, until a place could be provided for him in their household. The couple set up home at Strutton Ground, Westminster, near the Artillery Ground. On 26th June 1690 their first child, William, was baptised at the Savoy Chapel in the Strand. Only one of three chapels in the Savoy Precinct, built as the Hospital of the Savoy circa 1500, survives today. The site of the German Lutheran Chapel, established by 1690 to provide for the new Royal Household, was cleared for development in the 1820s.

On 16th February 1691 a Royal Warrant appointed Conrad the youngest Groom of Ewry, an office in the Lord Steward's department of the Royal Household to provide clean linen and fresh water for the royal table. The Gentlemen of the Ewry had a fee on every yard of material bought for tablecloths or napkins and had the right to claim the fees for their own use. On 6th January 1698 Conrad was promoted to Second Groom of Ewry, finally becoming Groom of Ewry on 3rd July 1702.

Life at Court did not provide the excitement and extravagances of the earlier Stuart times but Conrad and Dinah would have had a comfortable lifestyle. London continued to expand as a city of wealth and influence, despite the ravages of the great fire of 1666 and the expenses of the continuous wars with France. A rapid rebuilding programme in the city to hold trade, wealth and skills together was virtually complete, as was the rebuilding of St Paul's Cathedral and the City churches. The Bank of England was established in 1691 and money for the European War debt was raised by excise duty on liquor. A Jewish influx in the latter part of the century increased the numbers of goldsmiths, bankers and merchants.

In November 1693 Conrad and Dinah's second child, Dinah, was baptised at the Savoy Chapel, followed by John, baptised August 1695, Charles, baptised January 1699, twins Anna and Philip, baptised March 1700 and Peter, baptised October 1700. For the purpose of this history of the Roupell family, only the two older sons, William and John, are significant. William, the elder, was the forebear of the Roupells of Charlton, the successful branch of the family still extant, while the second son John was the forebear of the ill-fated Roupells of Lambeth. The parallel evolution of the two families provides an interesting comparison.

Three years after his promotion to Groom of Ewry, Conrad died in Germany on 31st December 1705. Probate was granted to his widow Dinah, who then appears to have removed to an address in the parish of St James. Dinah received a widow's pension of £40 per annum from the Lord Steward's department of the Royal Household. Life with seven children to support could not have been easy and, to supplement her pension, Dinah dealt in the buying and selling of lace.

In 1713 or soon after, her eldest son William married Sarah Whitfield, the wealthy widow of Walter Whitfield, MP for New Romney from 1704 until his death in January 1713. Sarah was at least twenty-five years older than William, who was twenty-three in 1713. She already had a daughter Anne, who was married to the Earl of Islay, second son of the Duke of Argyll, whose principal home was Ham House, Richmond. Pathetic letters exist, written in 1723 by Sarah Roupell to Sir Hans Sloane soliciting his medical skills to help her daughter, who was seriously ill. Lady Islay died the day before her mother, Sarah Roupell, in Kensington. Both were buried at St Mary Abbot's Church, Kensington, on 7th and 8th September respectively, leaving William a widower, no doubt a wealthy one. A few weeks later, on 13th November

1723, William, aged thirty-three, of the parish of St James Westminster, was married by licence to Anne Towley of Chelsea, aged twenty-five, at the Chapel Royal, Whitehall. Their son George was born in 1725.

In October 1716 Philip, one of Dinah's younger sons, became apprenticed to a coach-maker. In October 1721, another son Peter was gazetted as an Ensign in the 38th Foot (S. Staffs) Regiment, then in the West Indies. Dinah's second son John married Patience, their son John being born in 1733.

The Savoy in 1650

It seems that, although the family may have been well-connected, Dinah found it difficult to live on the proceeds of her lace business and her pension. It appears that small-scale money-lending could well have been another source of her income. Sometime before 1718, she apparently had available sufficient money to lend the considerable sum of £500 to her friends, sisters Mary and Alice Connock. Soon after this, the sisters asked Dinah for another loan of £60, which she was unable to provide. She arranged for the sisters to obtain the money from Sebastian Van der Eycken, a mutual friend, the Low Dutch Chaplain to George I at St James's Palace, on the security of the estate of Major Connock, deceased brother of the sisters, his executrices. Dinah unwisely signed two Promissory Notes, on or before 13th May 1718, for £35 and £25, in effect making her guarantor.

Apparently nine months after signing the Notes, bankruptcy proceedings were started against her. On 18th March 1721 in the London Gazette, Dinah, described as a Widow and Lace-woman, was declared bankrupt, with effect from 7th April, the certificate to cover the following seven years. She was thus protected by law via the bankruptcy proceedings from responsibility for the debt.

Late in 1725 she visited Holland. She stayed in Dort with her niece who was married to an English wine merchant, John Sayers. On 5th March 1726, Van der Eycken used his influence to have her arrested for the debt as she was no longer protected by the English bankruptcy law. She spent seven months in prison before bail was arranged. On 5th October 1726 John Sayers stood bail for Dinah's release, agreeing she should not leave his house until she repaid the debt or provided security. She was released and escaped with him to England. She appears to have been arrested again in Dort the following year. Her perhaps risky visits to Holland were probably in order to replenish her stock of lace, rather than solely to visit her niece.

In March 1736 Chancery proceedings were instituted by Dinah against Van der Eycken for wrongful arrest and imprisonment and to restrain him from taking action against John Sayers on account of the broken bail. By this date, nine years after the last arrest and some eighteen years after the original loan, Dinah was at least in her sixties and still suffering from its repercussions.

A large and closely written document lodged in the Public Record Office, dated 10th March 1736, giving Van der Eycken's statement, makes fascinating reading. He denied a friendship with either Dinah or the sisters. He denied knowing how long Dinah had lived or traded in the parish of St James, stating that he remembered neither living nor residing in the parish himself, other than attending to his duties at the palace as Chaplain, first to King George I then to George II. He admitted living in or around London and St James's for some twenty-three years and at the time of the proceedings being resident at Scotland Yard. He admitted some knowledge of the sisters but denied any particular correspondence or friendship. He agreed he had been acquainted with Dinah before 1718 but denied any knowledge of a loan to the sisters. He stated that neither sister had requested or obtained a loan for themselves from him or from Dinah with his endorsement.

His account alleged the loan had been made to Dinah. He stated that two Promissory Notes dated 13th May 1718 for £35 and £25 were given after Mary Connock had pleaded with him to lend Dinah £60 to save her from a pressing demand resulting from trouble in the lace trade. Mary had assured him that he would not suffer from endorsing the notes when repayment was due. He said he had been unwilling that his name should be made use of and refused to comply. However Dinah, having become friendly with his wife Henrietta, and knowing her influence over him, had applied to her to use this influence which he had been unable to resist. He therefore, with Mary Connock, endorsed the loan to Dinah. He alleged that she had declared herself bankrupt to avoid repayment of this loan, rather than as a result of business problems. He had arranged the £60 loan from a Thomas Chauvin. Because the debt had not been repaid he was held responsible and in June 1719 was arrested for the debt and the interest incurred and imprisoned for several days. He was released when Chauvin discovered that it was not in his power to recover the money from Dinah. Settlement of costs was fixed at £73 7s, due by 1724. Still unable to redeem the debt, he was again imprisoned for several days around 22nd March 1724. Unfortunately for him, he was only able to submit copies of the Notes as he said he had lost the originals. Unfortunately also, there were no witnesses to back his account as both his wife and Mary Connock had since died.

Van der Eycken then went on to state he had been unable to trace Dinah for several years until late 1725 or early 1726, when he had been informed she had fled to Holland to avoid her creditors. He was told that she had been living in Dort for some considerable time so he sent information and instruction to cause her arrest on 5th March 1726. He did not know how long she was in custody before John Sayers raised bail. He said he had not previously requested security from her guarantors in England because he had not known her whereabouts. He neither knew nor believed that Dinah had ever loaned the Connock sisters £500, but he knew that they had absconded from their abode several years ago. He stated he had suffered considerably because of Dinah.

Shoe Lane in 1823

In a statement dated 26th May 1736 Dinah denied his allegation that she had escaped to Holland to avoid repayment by pointing out that Van der Eycken had known her and the sisters for many years and had always known of her whereabouts, both in London and Holland. She stated she had lived in the parish of St James for over twenty years. Friends in London, Thomas Pressley of Whitecross Street, Cripplegate, distiller, and Roger Llewellyn of Ludgate Hill, coffeeman, had provided the required security for her in this country, and still did so. Van der Eycken had consented to stop proceedings in 1726 because of her bankruptcy immunity. In the eight years since she had returned from Dort she had lived in the parish of St James, then for a while in Kensington, then later in Brentford, Middlesex. She thought all proceedings against her in Holland had stopped. She questioned why, if she was in his debt, he had not declared himself as a creditor at her bankruptcy proceedings. She suggested he had not done so because she was telling the truth.

Ruling regarding the wrongful imprisonment appears to have been given in Dinah's favour because another action on 21st June 1737 was brought by Van der Eycken to avoid paying costs. He averred that her further arrest on 31st May 1727 had been because she was guilty of Contempt of Court by breaking Dutch law when she broke bail and escaped to England in 1726 and the costs against this arrest were not therefore his responsibility.

Dinah probably lived with or near to her eldest son William in Kensington and then in Brentford. After his appointment to Edinburgh in 1730, she apparently went to live with her second son John, living with his wife Patience and son - also named John - in Shoe Lane, Holborn. She died just three years later and was buried on 22nd November 1740 at St Andrew's Church, Holborn. Her estate was administered to her son John on 1st January 1741.

In October 1737, Mary was born to John and Patience and baptised at St Andrew's Church, followed by William, baptised in March 1740. Another son was born and baptised at St Andrew's in January 1743. He was also named William, a common practice, or perhaps because the William baptised three years earlier had died in infancy.

John Roupell of Shoe Lane was recorded as paying tax on premises in Bangor Court, Shoe Lane, at least from 1740. In 1752 he was listed as a jeweller on Ludgate Hill, a centre for goldsmiths, paying tax on premises in Dolphin Court. As the main thoroughfare between Westminster and the City, Fleet Street and Ludgate Hill contained fashionable shops, clubs and businesses, but the surrounding area was generally run down. The Fleet ditch, the filthy open sewer used to deposit rubbish from both Smithfield and Farringdon markets, was not filled in until the 1760s. Being outside the City boundary and near three prisons, Bridewell, Newgate and the Fleet, crime and business dealings occurred in close proximity. Farringdon Street, built over the Fleet ditch in 1737, was named after a goldsmith.

Life for John Roupell must have been very different from his childhood in Court circles. Shoe Lane was a narrow winding street in a decaying area. Bangor Court had once been the grand town house of the Bishops of Bangor but, by the time of the Roupell occupancy, it appears to have been divided into separate dwellings and was surrounded by a conglomerate of buildings in varying states of preservation. Shoe Lane, Field Lane and Saffron Hill were well-known for their bull and bear baiting and cock pits until the 1835 Cruel Sports Act caused their decline. Charles Dickens was to use this area to locate Fagin's den in *Oliver Twist*.

It is interesting to speculate how the future Roupell wealth originated. Dinah appears to have dabbled in money-lending; her son John, as a jeweller, must have had some knowledge of precious metal dealing.

Bangor House in the 18th century

John's eldest son, the second John, aged twenty-six, made a perhaps unsuitable marriage to Mary Canter, just sixteen, the daughter of John and Rebecca Canter of nearby Bishop's Court, off Old Bailey, on 14th October 1759 at St Pancras Old Church. Both were recorded as resident in the parish at the time. Mary, being illiterate, signed her name with a cross on the parish record. Two months later, on 23rd December 1759, John's father, the first John, aged sixty-four, was buried at St Martin Ludgate; his widow Patience continued to pay tax on the Dolphin Court premises.

On 16th April 1761 the third John, son of John and Mary, now recorded as living in nearby Field Lane, was baptised at St Andrew's Church. In May 1762, his grandmother, Patience, was buried at St Martin Ludgate alongside her husband. A few months later in February 1763 her son William, only in his early twenties, was buried in the same vault. In November of the same year Thomas Edward was born, second son of John and Mary, being baptised at St Martin's; followed by an infant death, James Cecil, two years later; then a daughter, Mary Rebecca, baptised at St Martin's in November 1766.

In 1766 the second John Roupell was still paying tax on Dolphin Court but the following year he was recorded in Stonecutter Street, which joins Shoe Lane and Farringdon Street. It is not known how he made a living - perhaps he carried on his father's jewellery business. He died in 1777, aged forty-four, and was buried on 24th December at St Bride's Church, Fleet Street. His widow Mary continued to occupy Stonecutter Street until she married a widower, Timothy Plaw, at St Andrew-by-Wardrobe, Blackfriars, in October 1783.

St Andrew's Church, Holborn in 1838

On 30th May 1781 the third John, aged twenty, made an advantageous marriage at St Bride's to Catherine Brand, aged 22, daughter of Thomas Brand, a wine merchant of Apps Court, Walton-on-Thames. Their only child Richard Palmer Roupell was born on 21st February 1782 and baptised a month later at St Bride's.

In November 1796 a lease on the area which was to become Roupell Street SE1 is recorded, and could well mark the date that John, Catherine and their son Richard Palmer Roupell moved across Blackfriars Bridge to set up their home and manufactory near the south bank of the Thames, in Southwark and Lambeth. Since the opening of Blackfriars Bridge in 1769, industry on this section of the south bank had expanded rapidly. By 1800 London, as a major port, industrial and business centre, was a thriving city. With a population of one million within a four mile radius of the City centre, London was the largest city in the world and its port handled 80% of the country's imports and 70% of its exports. Astute men of business made fortunes.

Before following John and Richard Palmer Roupell to Lambeth, it is interesting to trace the antecedents of the Roupells of Charlton who, at the height of William Roupell's notoriety as a convicted forger, were listed in Burke's Peerage in 1863, with a family seat at Chartham, Kent, and the motto 'Fidèle'.

William Roupell, eldest son of Conrad and Dinah, in 1730 became Inspector General of the Out Ports in Scotland and Collector of Salt Duties at Preston Pans, Edinburgh, probably through the influence of his friend John, Duke of Argyll, related by marriage to his step-daughter Anne. William's income of £130 per annum was over three times that of his mother, Dinah. In 1739 he refused to renew this appointment at this salary.

Blackfriars Bridge under construction in 1768

His son George emigrated to South Carolina USA in 1742 and, the following year, was appointed Searcher of Customs at Charleston. Again the Duke of Argyll, who owned property here, must have been influential. In 1753, both at the age of twenty-eight, George Roupell and Elizabeth Prioleau married. Descendants of a 16th century Doge of Venice, Elizabeth's family had founded the Huguenot church in South Carolina; and it is clear that the marriage was another advantageous alliance. The couple lived in Tradd Street, Charleston, and had three surviving children, their son George Boone, born in 1762, being of consequence to this history.

George Boone Roupell aged 18
Portrait by John Singleton Copley RA

By 1775 George Roupell was Deputy Postmaster General for the Southern District of North America, the British Forces having gained control after the American War of Independence in the mid-1760s. Benjamin Franklin held the same position for the Northern District. George now owned a plantation, which he named Rupelmonde, presumably after the place of the same name in Belgium. After he refused to sign an oath of allegiance to the new United States, he lost his job. Benjamin Franklin signed and went on to become President. For a while George served as Secretary of State in St Augustine, Florida, under General Grant's administration.

In 1777, after the rebellion of the American colonies, when his Custom House had been shut by violence and he had been imprisoned, George Roupell returned to England for three years. During this period his eighteen-year-old son, George Boone Roupell, had a full-length portrait painted by the American artist John Singleton Copley RA. Copley's son studied Law with George Boone. Later, by then Lord Lyndhurst, he gave the portrait to George Boone. It stayed in the family until 1977. George Boone remained in England after his father's return to Charleston. His father died in 1794; his mother in 1811.

George Boone Roupell's sister, Anne, married Robert McCulloch, who had first met their father George Roupell in Charleston. The McCullochs lived at East Combe House, Charlton, in the county of Kent. The house had originally been built in 1710 on land leased by Royal Assent to a captain (Conrad?) of the vessel which brought William of Orange to England, as a reward for his services. George Boone Roupell was called to the Bar in 1790, and three years later, aged thirty-one, he married his childhood sweetheart, Frances Browne McCulloch, presumably his brother-in-law's sister. They had nine children, the first five of whom were born in Lambeth at their new home Marlborough House, Kennington Road (extant), built about 1787. The three older children were baptised at the parish church of St Mary, Lambeth, between 1795 and 1799.

By 1803, George Boone Roupell's chambers were listed at Pump Court, Middle Temple, at about which time the family moved to Cherry Tree House, Charlton. A further four children were born to them there. By 1808 he had bought his country estate, Chartham Park, East Grinstead, where he built a new house. By 1816, through convenient marriages and further purchases, the Roupells owned land in Charlton on the slopes between the present Charlton Lane and Victoria Way and a marshy area fronting the river. After the coming of the railway over their land in 1848, the industrial and housing development commenced in 1850.

Marlborough House

In 1831 George Boone was appointed Master of High Chancery, with an address in Welbeck Street. In 1836 the Roupell wealth was further increased by the sale of the Rupelmonde plantation in Charleston. The plantation and African slaves were sold for $65,000; the house being worth about $7,000. George Boone Roupell died in January 1838, aged sixty-five, less than three years after the death in Lambeth of his second cousin, John. He was buried at St Luke's Church, Charlton, where later were to be buried his wife and two of their sons.

Surely it is reasonable to assume that John Roupell's ambition was at least in part fired by rivalry with, and perhaps the influence of, his more exalted cousin? Marlborough House was within walking distance of Bear Lane where John established his business, and nearer still to the future Roupell Street area, both of which appear to have been acquired by John by 1800, shortly after George Boone Roupell moved into the area. John Roupell's first major land purchase, the farmland on Brixton Hill, was made in 1810, two years after his cousin had obtained Chartham Park. The fortunes of both families seem to be bound up with a drive for land ownership, success and public acclaim.

Coincidentally, even closer to Marlborough House was the Lambeth Vestry Hall (extant) where William Roupell M.P for Lambeth was to start his political career and meet his downfall, thirty years after George Boone Roupell became Master of the High Court of Chancery.

THE ROUPELLS OF ROUPELL STREET

Scrap Metal and Property 1796 - 1856

Around 1800, John Roupell, his wife Catherine and their son Richard moved south of the river Thames. Little evidence remains to give an accurate picture of the characters of the family and the motivation which drove John Roupell to be a man of substance by the time of his death in 1835, however it is pertinent to the story of the Roupells of Lambeth to interpret clues to account for the rapid rise and fall of the family fortunes.

By 1800, John's second cousin, George Boone Roupell, at thirty-eight a year younger than himself, had settled with his young family in a fine home, Marlborough House, designed by the architect Michael Searles on Kennington Road, a fashionable part of Lambeth. Recently called to the Bar with chambers in the Middle Temple, he was a successful lawyer and well established in Society. His family connections were impeccable. By 1808 he had purchased Chartham Park in East Grinstead and by 1816, via his wife's family, he owned land in Charlton, Kent (now London SE7).

In contrast, John Roupell, although probably fairly wealthy, had grown up in much poorer surroundings, with an ill-educated mother and a father whose sources of income were in trade, probably connected to his father's jewellery business, and as leaseholder of various rented properties in the Holborn area. Whatever the relationship was between the two cousins, they surely must have had knowledge of each other. For a time they lived near each other and some of their land buying activities show a marked similarity.

John's marriage at the age of twenty to Catherine Brand, two years older, at St Bride's Church, Fleet Street on 30th May 1781, seems to have been an advantageous match. Four years later Mary Rebecca, John's eighteen-year-old sister, married Catherine's brother James Brand, a hearth rug manufacturer. Catherine, the daughter of Thomas Brand of Apps Court, Walton-on-Thames, a wine merchant, and his wife Mary, née Woodford, was born on 9th March 1759. Her family connection via her maternal grandmother Elizabeth Palmer, a rector's daughter, was remembered in her son Richard Palmer

Roupell's middle name. Family connections with Writtle, near Chelmsford in Essex, via her paternal grandmother, the daughter of a yeoman farmer, may explain the ownership of land in the area by her husband and son, part of which was to lead to her grandson William's appearance in Chelmsford Crown Court in 1863. In 1791 Catherine was a beneficiary of the will of her wealthy aunt Ann Osborne (née Brand), of Writtle, owner of a large estate.

Richard Palmer Roupell, born nine months after his parents' marriage, was their only child. According to his son William's testimony at his trial, Richard Palmer had an unhappy childhood relationship with his father, of whom he was frightened, a pattern he seems to have replicated with his children. Both John and Richard Palmer were noted for the energy and time they spent at work, to the exclusion of anything else. They were known for their astute business deals - and their dislike of spending money unnecessarily!

Exactly when the Roupells crossed Blackfriars Bridge to settle south of the river is uncertain. They still appear to be in Stonecutter Street in 1792 but, in a deed of 1880, reference is made to a 99-year lease on the future Roupell Street area in Lambeth, dated 18th November 1796, which is probably when John Roupell acquired it. In 1750 a path existed along the line of the present Roupell Street crossing the marshy area from a house on Cornwall Road to Broadwall. This was known as the Halfpenny Hatch from the toll paid for the use of it. By 1779 the land to the north of the famous Curtis's Botanic Garden had been acquired by the Curtis family. In 1789, because of atmospheric pollution, Curtis moved his garden to Kensington. Subsequently the freehold of seven acres of land around the Halfpenny Hatch was sold for £3,500. Apparently six months later it was sold on for £8,000 to John Roupell, which suggests that he became the landowner around 1792, the year after his wife Catherine received her bequest from her aunt. Was the leap in purchase price an indication of the rapidly rising cost of land, or was it one of John's less successful deals? How much did Catherine contribute? He continued to collect the toll at least until Roupell Street was laid out in about 1825.

The first specific reference found to John Roupell in the area is on 21st August 1810 when he began his purchase of land at Brixton Hill. His address was given as Cuper's Bridge, the riverside area north of Cuper's Gardens, once a mid-17th century pleasure garden replaced by 1762 with Beaufoy's Wine and Vinegar factory. The site today is covered by the surrounds of the Waterloo Bridge roundabout adjacent to the Roupell Street area. In 1823 John was recorded paying rates on a house, factory and land in Cornwall Road.

Horwood's map c1800 shows the distinctive square shot tower, down which molten lead was dropped into a tank of water to form gunshot, a manufactory on the river front and an iron foundry just to the south in Cornwall Road. It has yet to be proved which was the Roupell factory. John was recorded as a lead smelter in 1819, but in Bear Lane. Where was he before this? His son Richard was the first Roupell to appear in a trade directory, in 1817, listed as an engine-maker and millsmith. He could well have worked at the iron foundry.

The Bear Lane factory was certainly established before 1820, as John was listed then as a lead smelter of 16 Cross Street and as a smith at 33 Bear Lane. By 1826 he was recorded as an anchorsmith of Bear Lane and a lead-ash smelter of Cross Street. Two years later he was listed as a lead smelter of Gravel Lane and a wrought iron manufacturer of Bear Lane. By 1834 these were described as a lead works and an iron foundry. Other premises in the area were acquired over the years, including Glasshouse Yard, Gravel Lane, in 1821, later listed as Dyers Buildings, and premises at the junction of the present Ewer and Lavington Streets. Similar listings continued until Richard's death in 1856.

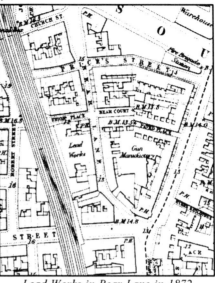

Lead Works in Bear Lane in 1872

By the early 1800s the area was rapidly becoming industrialised, with factories polluting the atmosphere and low-class dwellings quickly erected over the former marsh land to house the workers. Many of their employers lived nearby but perhaps had a country home a few miles south on higher ground. The Roupells, however, lived only over the office and by the yard in Cross Street, just a few minutes' walk across Blackfriars Road to their factory and premises in the triangular patch of land formed by Bear Lane, Gravel Lane (now Great Suffolk Street) and Price's Street. Their country home, Aspen House, was not built until 1839, after John's death.

In February 1820 an account of The King v Roupell from the Court of Chancery appeared in *The Times* newspaper. This concerned John Roupell's lead manufactory in Price's Street. Roupell had previously been convicted as a nuisance for showering surrounding properties, gardens and inhabitants, including the night watchman, with arsenic from the smoke issuing from his factory chimney. Despite his offer to heighten the chimney and his assertions that his business would be ruined should he be forced to stop lead-smelting, his plea was rejected and he was instructed to cease. This no doubt explains the subsequent variety of directory entries describing his business. However he was elsewhere usually described as a lead-smelter so perhaps the ban was short-lived.

John's address was first given in 1819 as Cross Street, now Meymott Street, off Blackfriars Road, just in Southwark. John, Catherine and their son Richard Palmer lived here for the rest of their lives. It is perhaps not difficult to imagine the atmosphere in the small house in Cross Street, containing John's office and a factory yard at the back, lacking any of the luxuries their increasing wealth could afford. It is not surprising that the inability of John, and then of his son, to relate to their children should be a contributory factor to William's subsequent downfall. Richard Palmer's relationship with his mother must have been better, but he was sufficiently wary not to marry until he had secured his inheritance after her death. There is no indication that she was ever aware of her four grandchildren.

Possibly influenced by his cousin George Boone Roupell, now the owner of Chartham Park in Kent, John Roupell bought farm land, in what was then Surrey, on Brixton Hill in the parish of Streatham. He and his son appear to have owned both the future Roupell Street and Roupell Park land for some twenty years before housing development started around 1825 and 1835 respectively. By 1825 John was sixty-four and his son forty-three, so it may safely be assumed that Richard Palmer was the driving force behind the development of the estates.

John's intention seems to have been to acquire property to rent. That part of his income was so derived is borne out by the fact that he was still landlord of premises in Shoe Lane and around Cross Street at his death. In 1823 he was recorded as landlord to six tenants in Princes Square (now Cleaver Square?) behind Marlborough House, where his cousin George Boone had lived until twenty years previously. He also paid rates on a house and yard in Broadwall, probably their Cross Street home, as well as the house, factory and land in Cornwall Road. In 1828 he is rated for the house in Cross Street, seven houses in Broadwall and a house and manufactory in Bear Lane.

In about 1824 Roupell Street, Lambeth, was laid out and development started. Small, closely packed terrace houses, dwellings for workers, rapidly appeared, their occupants paying rent to John Roupell. By 1829 the Roupell buildings were listed as twenty-seven houses and thirty-five buildings.

In June of that year fire entirely destroyed one of the new houses in Roupell Street, and an adjacent house considerably damaged, despite the efforts of officers from the Palladium and West of England fire-offices. An enquiry found that Roupell, contracted to finish both houses within a given time, had employed men to work beyond the usual hours. A pot of pitch boiled over, setting fire to wood, and the workmen were lucky to escape injury. Neither building was insured.

By 1830 two batches of thirty-four and thirty-seven houses were complete. At John's death in 1835 there were seventy-three houses; by 1839 the number had increased to eighty-two. The streets were named after the family: Roupell, John

(Theed), Catherine (Whittlesey east) and Richard (Whittlesey west). Because of the abundance of John, Richard and Catherine Streets representing other families in the area, these were changed later in the century to their present names, given in brackets.

Roupell Street, Lambeth, in 1989

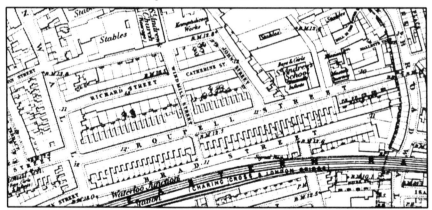

Richard, Catherine, Roupell and neighbouring Streets in 1872

Between 1810 and 1819 John Roupell paid a total of about £12,000 for parcels of land from the estate of the late Lord Chancellor of England, Lord Thurlow, who had owned much of the land that is now Brixton Hill, Streatham Hill, Tulse Hill and West Norwood (then in Surrey, now in the London Borough of Lambeth). The Thurlow estate appears to have been difficult to sell because of its large size and its location. Most of it was undulating farm and woodland with panoramic views and it was over four miles from the City, but it was possibly too near and too unfashionable to attract the rich looking for a country home. Although there were some fine old country houses situated in parkland in the area, most of the early 19th century development consisted of large houses lining the main roads. It was not until the 1840s that significant building started, accelerating rapidly a decade later with the coming of the railways.

John Roupell bought the future Roupell Park, Streatham, in lots over a period of nine years. In 1810 he bought land for £550, two small Brixton Hill allotments for £500 and part of the Knight's Hill estate for £1,916 5s (near Norwood Road/Tulse Hill today). The following year he added property to the north of his land at the top of Brixton Hill, buying two cottages, formerly part of Brixton Hill Farm, and for £1,720 another section of the Knights Hill estate. In 1813 he paid rates on two areas of land of some fourteen and eleven acres. These are recorded as being at Water Lane, Brixton Hill, but there is no evidence that they were other than the land at Streatham. In 1818 John paid rates on a barn and land, and Richard Palmer Roupell bought for £5,549 (plus £86 14s for timber) more land in trust for John. The following year John bought for £1,650 several more pieces of land totalling some thirty acres.

John now owned the complete area between the present Brixton/Streatham Hill and Norwood Road, along Christchurch and Palace Roads, the boundary being to the north and south of each, stretching along Leigham Vale and behind Kingsmead Road at the Norwood end, and between Holmewood Road and the bus depot on Streatham Hill. He appears to have leased much of it as farmland. No other transactions occurred during his lifetime apart from two sales of land in 1829: one for the building of the Union Chapel, later the Streatham Hill Congregational Church, and the other for the building of the Royal Asylum of the St Anne's Society, now the site of Pullman Court. Additionally a plot adjacent to the Union chapel was sold for £595 in 1832 to Edward Day of Clapham, a schoolmaster. It is tempting to suggest that it was Richard Palmer Roupell who influenced his father to sell these sites and thereby pioneer the sale of land for buildings which would add to the prestige of the Roupell name. Estate records show that the Roupells sold land in several areas during this period for the building of a church or a railway, or both, courting references to both God and Mammon!

Their next land purchase was in 1820 when Richard bought the fourteen years unexpired lease on five acres off the Wandsworth Road, bounded by the present Hartington Road. By 1824 a variety of building leases had been sold by Richard and, between then and 1830, terraced housing appeared along Spring Grove, Place and Terrace and on Simpson and Neptune Streets.

Judging by the business associates named on various documents concerning the Roupells, it is apparent that they were part of a network of influential contacts. By now Richard Palmer Roupell, listed in directories as a gentleman, had met Sarah

Crane, a carpenter's daughter. How long he had known Sarah is unclear. At William's later trial it was suggested that Richard Palmer had seduced Sarah when a young girl, but there is no evidence of this. By the time she was pregnant with their first child, Sarah was twenty-nine and Richard Palmer was forty-three. Although there was a fourteen year age gap, Sarah was hardly a young girl. Perhaps after a long relationship, when she had anticipated marriage, she had agreed to the liaison after it became apparent that this was unlikely and that she was past the usual marriageable age. It appears that both her parents by then were dead, suggesting that maybe Sarah needed the security Richard Palmer could provide for her.

Sarah, daughter of Thomas Crane and Sarah (née Harvey) was born on 9th September 1796 in the village of Stoke Ash, Suffolk, off the main Ipswich - Norwich road. The Harveys were local to the area. Sarah's two sisters, Maria and Leah, were later to live in London. Richard and Sarah's first child John was born on 5th January 1826. He was baptised at St Pancras Church. He was recorded with the surname left blank but both parents were named. The address given was Clarendon Street (now Grove?), Somers Town. His aunt, Leah Crane, was baptised two years later, at the age of twenty-three, at All Souls Church, Langham Place, her father being recorded as deceased.

By the time William was born on 7th April 1831, the family were living in a small house in Pitt Street, Peckham (now East Surrey Grove). Their father visited his family on Sunday, returning to Cross Street on Monday morning. Sarah was born on 21st October 1833 and baptised at St Giles's Church, Camberwell. Emma was born on 10th February 1837, but neither she nor William were baptised until after their parents married. William, at his trial, stated that he and his siblings were fearful of their father's reactions, implying a quick temper and unease in his children's presence. His involvement in his children's upbringing must have been minimal, Sarah being the major influence. Eleanor Wallet, later giving evidence, said that the children came to her for their schooling.

On 23rd December 1835 John Roupell died, aged seventy-five, and was buried at the newly built St John's Church, Waterloo, on 2nd January. His address was given as Roupell Street, in Lambeth, not as his home at Cross Street in Southwark. His estate was valued at £25,000, administered in favour of his son, Catherine having renounced her claim. The administrators were their son Richard

St John's Church, Waterloo c.1828

Palmer, W Webb, a cheesemonger of Blackfriars Road and G Comfort, a butcher of Farringdon Market. Death duties of £126 9s 11d were paid. An ironic comparison is the £50,000 debt inherited by Queen Victoria on her accession the following year. On 7th May 1836 Catherine made her will in favour of her son and from 1st June documents show a marked increase in his buying, selling and land development activity.

Land at Stapleford Abbots in Essex is first mentioned at this time, although it had probably belonged to John Roupell at least as long as Roupell Park, as a deed of November 1836 admitting Richard Palmer as his father's heir implies. Being located near to Catherine's family, its acquisition was probably through her connections. In December 1836 Richard started negotiations to buy Norbiton Park estate.

On 27th February 1838 Catherine died at Cross Street, aged seventy-eight, and was buried next to her husband in St John's churchyard. Their tombstone can still be clearly read, giving their ages, dates of death and the address 'Of Roupell Street'. Catherine left £12,000 to her son. Her will was proved in November. The value of bequests was given as £9,054 17s and death duties of £900 10s 11d were paid. Nine days after the will was proved, Richard Palmer Roupell and Sarah Crane were married at St Giles's Church, Camberwell, on December 6th 1838. Richard Palmer was aged fifty-four, Sarah forty-two, John twelve, William seven, Sarah five and Emma one.

At the 1862 trial, William Tarte a lead merchant of Tothill Street, Westminster, a friend of Richard Palmer's, attested that Richard had told him that his father was an eccentric character who would not have left him any property had he married. He told Tarte that he had a family by the person that he had been living with, but that his relations (probably his maternal cousins) had advised him to marry someone else. Tarte advised the opposite. The thought of starting a new family at fifty-four no doubt swayed his advice and Richard Palmer's decision.

On February 10th 1839, two months after her marriage, Sarah took her children to St George's Church, Camberwell, where William and Emma were baptised and John and Sarah, already baptised, were received into the church. Understandably this was an important event for Sarah, as she was now a respectably married woman. The same year Richard started building Aspen House on the Roupell Park Estate, and in October he sold land for the building of Christ Church, agreeing to build a road past this to connect Brixton Hill and Upper Tulse Hill. No doubt he was preparing his position in Streatham, although he continued to live in Cross Street until his death in 1856.

By 1840 Sarah and the children had moved from the obscurity of Peckham to Aspen House. Little did their new neighbours know that the first family of Roupell Park hid a secret that was, some twenty years later, to be revealed in national newspapers in one of the major scandals of the century.

THE ROUPELLS OF ROUPELL PARK

The Rise to Fame 1840 - 1857

By 1838, Richard Palmer Roupell, lead-ash smelter, smith and iron-turner of Bear Lane, Roupell Street, Lambeth, and Roupell Park, Streatham Hill, was recognised as a gentleman of the new Victorian Age, despite his commercial origins. His distant cousin, George Boone Roupell of Chartham Park and Charlton, was now Master of the High Court of Chancery. After the death of his father John Roupell, Richard's land buying accelerated and he started developing his country estate in Streatham. By now he owned fifty-five acres of arable and meadow land at the top of Brixton Hill. A plan exists of the estate in 1838, drawn later in 1855 and verified by the bailiff David Osbourne. Osbourne was recorded in the 1841 census as living in Roupell's cottage, probably that on the land adjacent to Aspen House, with his wife and five agricultural labourers. In January 1839, the ever-careful Roupell had the rates on his dwelling house reduced because he resided there only when farming his land. The 1840 tithe map shows him owning and occupying, at the junction of Streatham and Brixton Hills, a reservoir field, a meadow, an orchard and ground for building a house.

His new house, Aspen House, facing west, was situated close to the main road leading south through Streatham. Aspen House was smaller than other houses built at this time on Roupell Park, Richard Palmer's new position as lord of his estate no doubt being in conflict with his dislike of wasting money. From its position at the top of the hill, views from the back of Aspen House would have extended over fields towards the City. A large garden ending in an orchard was laid out behind the house. Immediately to the south of the house and garden was a path eventually leading to Norwood Road, beside fields and roughly along the line of the future Palace Road. At the other side of this path was more land separating Aspen House from the site of Boylands Oak, a large house to be built on the corner of the road leading to the site of Christ Church; the future Christchurch Road. The path through their land was to lead directly to Christ Church, soon to be built in an imposing position behind Aspen House. Although their house was comparatively small, the grounds were more extensive than other houses in the locality. The Roupell children had plenty of room to play out of sight of their neighbours, unlike their former home.

It is not difficult to imagine the changes in the lifestyle of Sarah Roupell and her children after their removal to Streatham. Aspen House may not have been an imposing mansion, but to Richard Palmer's family their new home must have appeared very large after the terrace house in Pitt Street. Their position as first family of Roupell Park must have seemed very strange. Perhaps they were far happier growing up in Peckham with friends and neighbours nearby, being brought up by their mother with the help of her day servant, Jane Woodleigh, and being taught by Eleanor Wallet. Their father, living in Cross Street during the week, must have seemed a very distant figure, having little immediate influence on their lives.

At first, Richard Palmer Roupell visited his family in Streatham twice a week, but this soon diminished to a visit from Saturday afternoon to Monday morning. Either he preferred his work to his children's company, or perhaps soon completed the business transactions bringing him to the area. The only legitimate child of the union, Richard, was born at Aspen House on 27th July 1840. Sarah's loyal servant, Jane Woodleigh, helped to deliver Richard and her friend, Eleanor Wallet, was there on the day of the birth. His father was then fifty-eight, his mother forty-three, John fourteen, William nine, Sarah six and Emma three. Shortly afterwards, in October 1840, his father apparently made a will in the new son's favour.

Within a year the lives of the four older Roupell children had changed markedly. From their relaxed, female-dominated lives in Peckham, they were now the children of a respected wealthy businessman, and were expected to behave as such. In Peckham their mother was known as Mrs Carter. It is unclear what surname was given to them, although on John and Sarah's baptismal records the Roupell name is recorded. Suddenly their mother was Mrs Roupell and they had to relate to a father they hardly knew. John and William were old enough to wonder and question. They now also had a brother whom their father appeared to favour above them. It is easy to speculate on the effect the circumstances of their birth and upbringing had on both boys.

Jane Woodleigh, the servant who had known the children all their lives, described John as being rather wild and said that his father later sent him abroad. She stated that although she saw little of Richard Palmer Roupell she knew that he was fond of his children. Mr Lord Huntley, the local doctor who delivered Richard, described John as unruly until he went to school. He then improved a little, but on leaving school his behaviour deteriorated so much that his father sent him abroad. Mr Huntley said that William, on the other hand, was a steady, studious young man.

William later denied allegations that John was a wastrel who had been sent abroad because he had stolen money to give to a woman. He had provided his brother with money to go to the Cape of Good Hope in South Africa because of John's deteriorating relationship with his father, to the extent that he had refused to see him or maintain him although he had no means of support. William described his father as a good, but eccentric, man who did not relate well to his children.

It is uncertain when John went to the Cape, but his distant Charlton cousin Thomas Boone Roupell, a civil servant with the East India Company and son of George Boone, visited the Cape in 1846, where his wife Arabella later published a book of water colours of Cape flowers. John would have been twenty then, and it seems quite possible that his journey was made at the same time. In a will of 1850 Richard Palmer apparently left John an allowance of £200 a year. At the age of thirty-five, on 28th November 1861, John died at an hotel in Adderley Street, Port Elizabeth, just months before William's downfall. He left effects valued at £10. His body was returned to England and buried in the family vault at the South Metropolitan (subsequently known as West Norwood) Cemetery.

Aspen House
Brixton Hill
c.1905

And what of their mother, Sarah? Throughout the Roupell story she remains very much in the background. It was said at the trial, without corroboration, that her liaison with Richard Palmer Roupell started when she was seventeen and he thirty-one. That their first child was not born until twelve years later does not seem to bear this out. She was described as a faithful companion and true-hearted woman. A carpenter's daughter, with limited education, judging from her signature, her father died some time before the birth of John. Her two sisters later lived in south London: Maria Watts, who had married an attorney closely connected by business to William Roupell, and Leah, who died of consumption in 1843, aged 38, at Aspen House. She was buried at the recently opened (1837) West Norwood Cemetery, apparently the first to occupy the Roupell family vault. One of Richard Palmer's first actions on settling at his country estate, it would seem, was to have secured the family burial plot - at one of the best locations at the top of the hill!

Sarah appears to have had a loving relationship with her children, but her relationship with their father could hardly have been close. After the birth of John at least, she was kept in a degree of comfort, but not luxury. She called herself Mrs Carter, keeping the initial of her surname Crane. According to later statements at the trial regarding their paternity, her children do not appear to have been known as Roupell. Her transition to an unfamiliar life-style at Aspen House, without the support of her husband, must have been very difficult. Her friend Eleanor Wallet and Jane Woodleigh both remained loyal to her, the former regularly visiting Aspen House and the latter continuing there as her servant. Neither she nor her children appear to have met Richard Palmer Roupell's relatives, friends or associates before their marriage; they probably met few of them afterwards. She saw him only once a week but, being totally involved with business affairs, he appears to have had no inclination to relate to other women or interfere with her domestic arrangements. One of her first actions after her marriage was to have her children baptised or received, but at St George's Church, Camberwell, and not at St Giles's, her usual place of worship. However, unlike Scottish law where marriage between natural parents would have automatically legitimised their existing children, she could do nothing else to erase the circumstances of their birth.

After his marriage, Richard Palmer Roupell continued to carry on his life and business in Cross Street as usual. He was now landlord of all eighty-two houses in the Roupell Street development, apart from the King's Arms public house. In January 1839 he secured the purchase of Norbiton Park estate, in present-day New Malden, between Kingston Road, South Lane, Thetford and Presburgh Roads, the farm house being south of Park Road.

On 19th April 1839 a meeting was convened to start a subscription list for the building of a new church at Roupell Park. Roupell donated £100. He sold the site for its building in October and agreed to build a new road going past the new church to connect Streatham Hill and Upper Tulse Hill, which had recently been laid out by Thomas Edwards. This was the start of Christchurch and Roupell Roads.

In August 1840 the foundation stone of Christ Church was laid by Archdeacon Wilberforce, son of William Wilberforce, of the anti-slavery movement. Designed by the twenty-six-year-old architect JW Wild in a Lombardo-Byzantine style, with its tall campanile visible for miles, the church was of unusual design and is of particular architectural interest today (Grade 1 listed). The building costs incurred between 1840 and 1843 totalled £6,562 8s and the architect's fees were £342 2s. In September 1840 Thomas Edwards offered to pay the building costs and donated three stained glass windows. On 14th November Christ Church was consecrated.

The surviving subscription list shows that Richard Palmer Roupell donated a further £100, while Thomas Edwards gave £400 and land to build the parsonage, bought from Roupell for £255 in March 1842. In that year Richard Palmer Roupell's subscription dropped to £20, perhaps because, the consecration procession being over, he no longer needed to secure an advantageous position for himself. Richard, aged five, was baptised at Christ Church on 2nd November 1845.

Christ Church, Streatham Hill, c.1905.

In November 1839, Roupell bought land in Thundersley, Essex, now on the outskirts of Southend, near Basildon. The farmland, later known as Thundersley Lodge Farm, lay on a rectangular site north of the present A13, west of the A129 and about a mile along the road leading to New Thundersley. The following year, in October 1840, he bought Trunk Farm, at the junction of Trunk Road and Southwood Lane in Yately, near Farnborough in Hampshire, for £3,266 9s 3d. In March 1841 he bought the twenty-one-year lease on a pottery and adjoining buildings in Fore Street, along the Lambeth riverside. In March 1842, he sold the land at Streatham Hill for the building of Christ Church parsonage and in July bought more land in Essex - Marsh Farm at Laindon. He also owned Bury farm at Great Warley, east of Laindon and south of Brentwood, east of the M25 and south of the A127 today. Shortly after this purchase a substantial new farmhouse was built adjacent to the old farmhouse.

An interesting observation on looking at plans of the Roupell estates is that most of them have a railway running through or alongside - Roupell Street, Roupell Park, Trunk and Norbiton Farms, in particular. Other known estates are sufficiently close to a railway to suggest a connection; evidence surely that an astute Richard Palmer Roupell was in the right place at the right time to benefit from the coming of the railways in the 1850s.

In 1843 he is listed as paying the following Lambeth sewer rates: in Roupell Street, seventy-two houses £59 12s; in John Street, ten houses £7 10s; in Catherine Street, eleven houses £8 5s; in Richard Street, six houses £3; the Broadwall factory £3 10s; in Princes Square, six houses £2 5s; and Roupell's buildings, consisting of forty-six houses, plus a yard and house, stable and yard. Also listed was the factory land in Southwark. In December he paid £1,239 for the enfranchisement of the fifty-five acres of Roupell Park, Streatham, considered a better foundation for development than copyhold after the Copyhold Commissioners Act of 1841.

By 1847, unlike his brother John, William had become interested in his father's property development. William was articled as a lawyers'clerk to Haslam & Rees from 1849 until 1854. Once qualified, his only recorded appearance in court as a barrister was in a law suit against his father contesting the toll levied at the Hatch House, Halfpenny Hatch. However his knowledge of the law later proved useful for other purposes. At that time William's allowance from his father was £1 a week, later rising to 25s, an amount William regarded as inadequate for the son of a wealthy gentleman. In 1850 his father apparently made a new will leaving the bulk of his estates - Norbiton Park, Roupell Park and Great Warley - to his ten-year-old son Richard. Early in 1850 William fraudulently mortgaged Norbiton Farm to Edward Whittaker. Although never admitted, it seems certain that William by then was well aware of his illegitimacy and at least suspected that his father's will was written in favour of his younger brother.

In 1851, the year the 'Crystal Palace' was built for the Great Exhibition in Hyde Park, the census lists at Aspen House: Richard Palmer (sixty-nine), a farmer, smelter and proprietor of houses and land; his wife Sarah (fifty-four); William (twenty), an articled clerk; Sarah (seventeen), a farmer's daughter; Emma (fourteen) and Richard (eleven), scholars at home; and one general servant. The rural picture conjured up of the farmer and his children seems rather at odds with reality. In 1852, James Harvie Linklater, a solicitor in the City who was to play an important part in the Roupell trial and later history, took a twenty-one year lease on the house adjacent to Aspen House, named Boylands Oak after Roupell's farm in Stapleford Abbots, Essex.

By 1853 William was in debt for £1,000 to his uncle Watts, the lawyer husband of his mother's sister Maria. At this point it is worth noting and questioning the relationship between William and Watts. He seems to have been very involved in William's business transactions from the start. Mention was later made at William's trial of a relative who was said to bear at least some responsibility for his downfall, but was never called as witness. It seems very likely that Watts was this person. He had been articled to an attorney named King, later of the firm Whittaker and King of Grays Inn; Edward Whittaker had first loaned William money in 1850. In 1853 William Roupell's forgeries started in earnest, but it seems that his debts first occurred in 1850 with the Whittaker-financed first mortgage on Norbiton Park and that Watts was at least instrumental in suggesting or arranging these loans, which were frequently via Whittaker. In August 1853 William obtained a further mortgage of £7,000 on Norbiton Park.

In September 1853 William was apparently given Roupell Park via a deed of gift from his mother. To obtain access to the relevant deeds to make forgeries for this 'gift', he told his father he needed them because he had been appointed a building trustee to the Unity Fire Assurance Company, a firm with a fund of £50,000 to invest in Roupell Park. His father, now seventy-one, accepted this story and agreed to rent the estate to the Company for £2,750 per annum, on condition that the mythical £50,000 was spent on its development. William received two advances of £1,000 from Whittaker on Roupell Park in November and December.

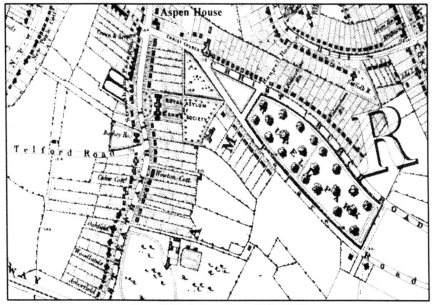

Roupell Park, Streatham Hill, 1861.

In 1854 Richard Palmer Roupell sold the site for the building of St Andrew's Church (bombed during WWII), between Prince's Street (Coin Street) and Cornwall Road. In January William received advances of £10,000 and £4,000 from Miss Louisa Douglas, on the security of land and a site on Christchurch Road, east of Garden Lane. He repaid £2,000 loaned to him in 1850 by Edward Whittaker on the security of Norbiton Park. In July 1854 Richard Palmer Roupell gave notice to the tenants of Roupell Park to make payments to his son William as attorney for the Fire Insurance lessees. In August the Fore Street property was leased to the noted potters, Doulton's of Lambeth, associates of the Roupells, for a drainpipe factory.

By 1855 William was pressed for money. He owed Whittaker £2,500 and the London & Westminster Bank £12,000, due for repayment in February 1856; Whittaker being his guarantor. No doubt in desperation, he advised his father to purchase a parcel of land from John Treadwell, a wealthy railway contractor, who lived on the Leigham Court estate adjoining Roupell Park to the south. He told his father the Unity Fire Assurance Company wished to rent this land for £250 per annum. His father agreed to buy it for £5,000 and handed over two cheques to his son for payment to Treadwell: the first an initial payment of £500 and later the second for the balance of £4,500. The first was used by William to settle a pressing debt, the second he paid into his personal account with the Bank of England.

Further transactions included supposed gifts from his father via Whittaker, with the privity of Watts: another £4,500 from Louisa Douglas on the aforementioned land at Roupell Park, and £30,000 from Barcley, Bever & Co on the Kingston and Great Warley properties in April. On 16th July William had copies made of the Norbiton Park deeds, returned them to the strong box, then forged a deed of gift via Whittaker, the conveyance being dated 28th July. A mortgage of £7,000 on this was raised from the unfortunate Louisa Douglas, of which he allegedly pocketed £2,000. A further mortgage on Norbiton Park was arranged from Whittaker, as was £2,500 on leases on houses in Roupell Park.

On 8th January 1856 he used a letter, supposedly from his father, but in his sister Sarah's handwriting, to grant himself the Warley property by deed of gift. William allegedly forged his father's signature and convinced a witness he was signing something else. The following day he obtained a mortgage on the Warley land for £12,000. In February another £3,500 was raised on the leases of houses in Roupell Park. He also raised a similar amount on the seven acres containing two cottages, previously part of the Leigham Court estate and leased to Roupell, but not yet paid for. In June a further £40,000 was raised on Roupell Park, followed by another £30,000 a month later and £5,000 on Norbiton Park.

By now he had fraudulently obtained some £100,000 and was clearly heading for disaster. Yet it was to be six more years before his deceptions were discovered. Only one solicitor questioned Richard Palmer Roupell's lack of involvement in William's deals - and that deal was quickly dropped.

In 1856 the opening of the West End of London and Crystal Palace Railway and the resultant ease of access to central London heralded the increasing popularity of the Streatham area and the future slow decline of Roupell Park (within less than thirty years) as a desirable place for the wealthy middle classes to settle. Roupell Park was soon to have two adjacent railway lines, with Tulse Hill and Streatham Hill stations situated nearby. However in 1856 it was still a considerable asset, made more so by William's carefully planned development. It was his management of money, more than his ambitions for Roupell Park, which was his downfall.

On 5th September 1856 Richard Palmer Roupell fell ill at Cross Street. His housekeeper immediately informed Sarah. For the following week she travelled to Cross Street each morning and was brought back by William, who arrived each evening at 7 pm to escort her home between 9 and 10 o'clock. On 12th of September Richard Palmer died, at the age of seventy-four, of 'natural serious apoplexy'. Sarah and William rushed to Cross Street.

William forging his father's will

Leaving his grief-stricken mother downstairs with the housekeeper, William went up to his father's death bed. Nearby was a strong box which he opened and found the will, dated 1850, which left the Kingston, Great Warley and Roupell Park estates to his sixteen-year-old brother Richard. Later accounts conflict. One states that it was only at this point that William realised his illegitimacy. Another suggests that he regarded these estates as his because he had concerned himself so much with their development and that he was certain his father's intention was to have bequeathed them to him. The reason this intention had not been fulfilled, William believed, was that his father would have had to spell out 'my son called William Roupell', the form of words used for illegitimate children, thus revealing his shameful secret. Whatever the truth, it would seem that William did indeed think he deserved recognition as the son who shared in his father's business undertakings. At worst, he had hoped to clear his financial difficulties either before his father's death or soon after.

William later admitted destroying the will at his father's bedside and forging another, dated 2nd September 1856, leaving everything to his mother with himself as executor. He was careful to sign his father's name with a quill pen and his own with his gold pen, as was customary. He took the will and had it witnessed by Henry

Muggeridge, a business associate of his father's who owned leases on several houses at Roupell Park. Muggeridge was an old man who would not be expected to live long.

Richard Palmer Roupell was buried in West Norwood Cemetery in the family vault which still bears his name on the side of the slab and looks over the Effra valley to Roupell Park. His will was proved in his widow's favour on 24th September, the estate being valued at £120,000. Subsequently it was easy for William to get his mother's consent to sell estates to raise more money.

He was now apparently a very wealthy young man. The valuation of the property on his father's death in 1856 gave these approximate values, in excess of £170,000:

Roupell Street estate	£50,000	Hop warehouses, Borough	£ 2,500
Kingston	£15,000	Wandsworth Road	£ 8,000
Warley, Essex	£12,000	Southwell	£ 4,500
Thundersley, Essex	£10,000	Trunk Farm, Hants	£ 4,500
Havering-atte-Bower	£ 7,500	Broadwall copyholds	£ 500
Lead works, Gravel Lane	£ 1,500	Aspen House	£ 400
Premises: Shoe Lane	£ 2,000	Roupell Park was later given a	
Bear Lane	£ 2,000	value similar to that of the	
Lant St. S'wark	£ 3,500	Roupell Street estate.	

By the same time William had received advances on the estate totalling £100,000, listed at the trial as follows:

Date of mortgage	Estate	Amount
1853 August 1st	Kingston	£ 7,000
1855 September 1st	Roupell Park house leases	£ 2,500
1856 February 1st	Roupell Park house leases	£ 3,500
	Great Warley	£12,000
1856 June 11th	Roupell Park	£40,000
1856 July 28th	Roupell Park	£30,000
	Kingston	£ 5,000

It is impossible to imagine how William expected to survive this financial chaos, how he could continue spending vast sums of money for six more years and why it was so long before his downfall. He benefited from the sound reputation of his father, the integrity of his lawyers and the involvement of many men of business who had much to lose. He apparently had the ability to inspire confidence, he had charm and, supposedly, money and success. He later showed considerable remorse, so how he could continue living a lie seemingly without a care is difficult to understand.

WILLIAM ROUPELL M.P.
Politics and Corruption 1857 - 1862

On Monday March 30th 1857, William Roupell, a week short of his twenty-sixth birthday, was one of two Liberal candidates elected to represent Lambeth in Parliament. *The Illustrated London News* described him as 'the son of a wealthy lead-smelter in the borough, who is said to have conveyed to his son on attaining his majority a few years since, landed property to the extent of half a million sterling. He now enters Parliament as an independent Liberal, pledged to further reform, ballot and the extension of the franchise; who desires to make the House of Commons the House of the People.'

To quote from Hill's *The Electoral History of Lambeth*, about this election : 'If the effect of the last election was to lower the moral tone of the electors, this election was still more damaging to the reputation of the borough. It revived corruption and dissipation, appealed to men's lowest passions, pandered to prejudices that quickened into actions, evoked a turbulent rowdyism that denounced the voice of reason and moderation, and, when the fumes of the election had cleared away, there was left behind a residuum of political degradation.'

The Borough of Lambeth first returned two members to Parliament in 1832, when it was enfranchised by the Reform Act. Its constituency, which included Camberwell, Peckham and Walworth up to the Elephant and Castle area, consisted of the £10 rate-paying householders. Its population in 1832 was about 155,000; in the 1851 census it was given as about 251,000; over the same period its registered electors rose from under 5,000 to over 18,000. By 1857, the electorate stood at about 20,000, some 8% of its total population. A large number of the residents of Lambeth lived in extreme poverty and were not entitled to vote.

It is not difficult to appreciate William Roupell's motivation to become the Member for Lambeth. He did not squander his wealth on fripperies, as was later suggested in the press. He used his money to buy the respect and standing in the community for which he craved. He had grown up first in an ordinary working class area in Peckham.

Then by the impressionable age of nine he was living in a sizeable country house on his father's estate. His father, until then a remote character, was a rich gentleman who expected his sons to behave as such and follow him into the family business. His brother John was a rebel and therefore rejected. William must always have been aware of his changing circumstances. He must have noted the difficulties his mother experienced in adapting to them. Sarah must have been very conscious of her own behaviour in public; whether she was acting and speaking correctly in her position as a gentleman's wife, usually without his support. She must have urged her children to remember their father's position and behave as he would wish.

William did as he was told. He worked hard at school, he trained in law as his father wished. As the young lawyer's clerk grew up he was almost certainly aware of the implications of his and Richard's births. He involved himself fully in his father's business, surely hoping that he could prove himself and be rewarded as his father's partner before his death. He saw the potential in his father's property, he tasted the riches and rewards possible in the circles of business and society in which he moved. He constantly strove to prove his worth and earn his father's praise and respect.

In 1855, the Metropolis Local Management Act came into operation and William Roupell was elected as a member of Lambeth Vestry, which met at the new Vestry Hall in Kennington Road (extant). He apparently attracted little attention and took no part in debates. It was rumoured he was rich, but his residence, Aspen House, was comparatively small. It is interesting to speculate on his father's reaction to his son's new position. Was William fulfilling his father's ambitions? Was he proud of him?

After the death of his father, he must have been panic-stricken. He had not achieved his aim to become a partner in the business and the will was not in his favour, perhaps because Richard Palmer did not want to publicise his shame by using the legal term necessary for illegitimate offspring, perhaps because he regarded Richard as his only legitimate child. William's bitterness and resentment must have been overwhelming. He had not the means to extricate himself from the financial mess in which he now found himself. He had hoped his inheritance would solve his problems. How much bad advice he received or whether he was over-confident and foolhardy is uncertain, but his need for recognition in society escalated after his father's death.

He began to be more prominent locally, rented an office in St James's Square, and soon expressed a wish to represent Lambeth in Parliament. He was regarded as a 'local young man of great expectations, possessing great ability and force of character'. He was educated for the Bar and it was supposed that education and training had overcome any disadvantages of his background. He saw himself as a benefactor of the poor of Lambeth, as encouraging the honesty and hard work of the working classes and, like other great Victorian philanthropists, using his money and influence to achieve these ends.

Roupell had, as yet, shown no aptitude for public speaking. Hill suggests it was difficult to form a correct judgement of his ability because he would occasionally make smart comments, but never speak at length or in detail. Once he started to make public addresses his limitations as a speaker were obvious, but his followers in Lambeth were prepared to applaud anything he said. He enjoyed oratory, he loved an audience, he had charm - and money.

The Hustings on Kennington Common at the Lambeth Election of 1857

On the evening of Wednesday March 11th 1857, at the Horns Tavern, Kennington Common, Roupell was introduced as a new candidate, after an address from the sitting MP William Williams, a London merchant and former MP for Coventry. The third candidate was a Mr Wilkinson. The next day his committee was formed and started immediate canvassing. He made a speech to his supporters explaining his principles. He pledged himself as a Reformer, "to support the ballot, extension of suffrage, equalisation of the poor rate, administrative reform, to uphold the honour of the country in connection with its foreign relations, to oppose compulsory church rates and support the reduction of public expenditure in order to abolish income tax."

With hindsight, there is much in his rousing speeches that is amusing, but at the time they indicated noble ideals and a promise of distinction and service to Lambeth.

Comparison with politics today is tempting. His first address to the electors started:

"Gentlemen, summoned by numerous and repeated calls to become a candidate for the representation of your Borough, I should have considered it a mark of disrespect to such a constituency, were I to refuse at once to place myself at your service. Connected with you by the closest ties, both by property and descent, I claim to represent your feelings, sympathies and interests, in a degree with which few others can compete. Although young in years, I have received a political and social training, which has rendered me a member of the most advanced section of the great Liberal party ....

"(There is) urgent necessity... (for) Administrative Reform carried into every section of our government departments, but more especially those which have shown themselves hopelessly tainted with the sins of lavish extravagance, glaring incapacity, and the greatest nepotism ...

"My connection with the working classes has deeply impressed upon my mind the necessity for the most liberal and comprehensive view of the education question, and I may be permitted to point with pride at my own personal efforts to carry out practically the principles I profess. I have not, however, confined my attention only to the rising generation, but have consecrated a portion of those goods with which Providence has endowed me to the advance of the social and physical well-being of the working man ..."

Roupell's speeches, written to appeal to as wide a range of opinion as possible, when considered within the context of his financial operations show either a self-deception, stupidity or inability to face reality which is quite amazing.

The Morning Advertiser quickly adopted his cause, on March 16th describing him thus: 'Mr Roupell is a young man of great public spirit. His sympathies are thoroughly with the people; and he uses the great wealth with which Providence has favoured him for the benefit of his fellow men. He is, besides, a resident in the borough - and our readers are aware how earnestly we have, for many years, urged on constituencies the propriety of returning local or resident candidates in preference to others, when they possess the general requisite qualifications. Mr Roupell's political opinions on the leading questions of the day are in perfect accord with those of the great majority.'

Over the next two weeks he attended many meetings and gave similar addresses to hundreds of people. His meeting in the Music Hall, Surrey Gardens, was described by *The Morning Advertiser* as being crammed to overflowing and at 8 o'clock the outer gates, at the ends of avenues leading to the grounds, had to be closed as more than eleven thousand people were present. Crowded meetings were also held at the Hawkstone Hall, north Lambeth, the Victoria Theatre (the Old Vic), the Camberwell Hall, Grove Lane, and Carter Street Hall where his placards 'Roupell, and No Income Tax' were first displayed.

Lambeth elections were exciting occasions. After the selection of candidates at the Horns Tavern, nominations followed on Kennington Common. Hundreds of people gathered before the hustings. Canvassers and 'boardmen' carrying placards swarmed everywhere; bands played, banners flew; comment and heckling mixed with shouts and jeers. Public houses were taken over as 'committee rooms', canvassers scattered refreshment tickets for free drinks, societies were subsidised to attract supporters. To quote Hill: 'Lambeth became the rendezvous of an election carnival.'

At the Kennington hustings on a sunny morning at 10 o'clock on Saturday 28th March, the nomination of three candidates took place. Mr Wilkinson arrived quietly; Mr Williams arrived in the middle of a solemn procession of supporters, flanked by attendants carrying banners; Mr Roupell, the rich young bachelor, arrived with a cavalcade of some twelve carriages, some of the occupants being ladies waving handkerchiefs.

Amidst much enthusiasm, his nomination was proposed by his friend Frederick Doulton, third son of John and brother to Henry Doulton of the Lambeth pottery family. Roupell was received with tremendous cheers which lasted two or three minutes. He repeated former speeches, stressing he wanted inefficient government officials, whose only qualification was their title, replaced by men of business. He emphasised that he would go to the House of Commons as a pledged friend of the working man, determined to improve conditions, shorten working hours and protect women and girls working in factories against excessive labour.

Doulton, nine years Roupell's senior and a previously unsuccessful candidate, gave him his full support. This aroused criticism from some who remembered Doulton's address to the electors of Lambeth in 1852 when he had criticised dishonourable, unfair campaigning involving lavish expenditure. His critics accused Roupell of far greater expenditure. It was suggested, but denied, that Doulton wrote some of Roupell's more important speeches. Although this may be unlikely, it is fairly certain that Roupell did not write them himself. Hill commented that it would have been better for both if they had never met. He suggested both needed guidance: Doulton because of his impetuosity and Roupell because of his guilty conscience. However he accepted that Roupell deserved pity as he was the victim of peculiar circumstances and powerful temptations, 'with no early training to enable him to resist'.

These verses, a popular form of campaigning in the press, give an idea of the supposed relationship between Doulton and Roupell:

MASTER ROUPELL AND HIS NURSE
There was a young lawyer in Lambeth did dwell.
He had a large fortune, as I have heard tell:
And he had a friend Doulton, a riverside swell,
Who liked to play 'first fiddle' uncommon well.

As Doulton was a-walking in the gardien one day,
This lawyer came to him and thus he did say:-
"Oh write my address for me - shew me the way -
And I'll stand for Lambeth both galliant and gay."

Said Doulton to Roupell: "How much will you spend?
And which way, young sir, do your principles tend?"-
"Of those and of money I think I've no end."
"Then, if that's it," says Doulton, "why, I'll be your friend.

"So first you must take all the houses about,
And post all the bills of that Wilkinson out;
And the men with your boards must continually shout -
'It's money that makes a man, that there's no doubt.'

"You must have public meetings and you must be tried
Before your constituents all far and wide.
And we'll ask you questions to put you aside,
But give you the answers first, all cut and dried."

So they started, the lawyer, the young golden calf,
And took in poor people with all sorts of chaff;
But others in Lambeth too witty by half,
When they heard what was doing, did nothing but laugh.

For says they: "Here's a youngster scarce out of his teens.
No-one knows what he's done, no-one knows what he means.
And as for his politics, which way he leans,
It aren't of no consequence 'cos of his means.

"He's like a cigar that's too green to be smoked.
He's like a young lady too green to be joked.
He's like a sweet baby that's easily choked,
With the tops and the bottoms improperly soaked.

"Not fit to be tried, like a bottle of wine,
That hasn't a crust, for it aren't had the time.
Put him back in the cellar and there let him fine,
And when he's a grandfather, perhaps he may shine.

"But the Borough this time has been bought and been sold,
No principles guided us now, as of old,
And when all the votes have on Monday been polled,
Shall we find that we worshipped a nugget of gold?"

On Monday, the day of the poll, the excitement was heightened by the activities of mounted messengers who, every half-hour, collected returns from polling places and galloped with them to the Central Committee rooms. Flags and banners were suspended from various houses and surrounding bands played. Teams with posters and placards abounded, extolling the merits and demerits of the rival candidates. A large, noisy but good-humoured crowd assembled. Roupell, described as wearing a theatrical fur-lined great-coat, arrived in an open carriage drawn by four grey horses, with outriders in livery. *The Morning Advertiser* reported he was followed by sixty carriages. *The Illustrated London News* reported several ladies rode in the carriages, some being remarkably pretty. A line of men carrying placards for Roupell were deployed, with military precision, in front of the hustings. An equestrian was described, enveloped in his placards from head to foot, who dashed backwards (on horseback!) during an important part of William's speech.

William Roupell, MP for Lambeth

By 4pm, he had polled an unprecedented 9,318 votes, a majority of almost 6,000 over the unsuccessful candidate. Williams polled 7,346 and Wilkinson 3,152 votes. Roupell and Williams were duly elected. The following day, a procession of carriages conveyed the committees to Kennington where the successful candidates addressed the huge crowds who had gathered in spite of the rain. *The Morning Advertiser* reported his speech as being 'a glorious triumph of liberty and truth over the modern system of time serving and hypocrisy'. Wilkinson alleged that money had won him the election; Roupell replied that he had spent "much under average".

This remarkable poll, which was said to have cost Roupell £6,000, aroused such suspicion that a Committee of the House was set up to inquire into his electioneering methods. It was alleged that Roupell had spent thousands of pounds on the working classes, influencing employers and corrupting voters. He was accused of opening over a hundred public houses under the pretence that committee rooms had been hired in them; also that he had hired two hundred paid committee men, some publicans, and three hundred and fifty canvassers. Roupell's agreed expenses were £2,610, more than three times that of his nearest rival. It was estimated as much more than this, some estimates being as high as £9,000. Whatever the truth, this is one indication of how William Roupell managed to spend so much money in such a short time.

Evidence from various witnesses was taken, including from a number of publicans. It was alleged that Roupell and Doulton had gone to the Surrey Canal Tavern and directed that more public houses should be opened in that area to encourage support. The Swan Tavern had been given £20, the Queen's Arms £18 10s, the Bee-Hive £64, the William IV £51, the Duke of Norfolk £52, and similar sums to others. Various other expenses were listed. Finally Roupell was sworn in, when he acknowledged incurring expenses of £4,504 6s 5d.

Fortunately for him, he was able to give evidence of bribery, showing that those who had drawn up the petition which led to the setting up of the Committee had subsequently offered to drop it, and give him a directorship in the South London Railway Company, if he would use his influence as MP to secure the passage of the relevant Act during the following year. He gave a graphic account of the meeting at the House when he had been propositioned. He stated that he had been tempted to kick the man who had made the offer. This was Mr Rhodes, a hop merchant of Brixton Road, chairman of one of Wilkinson's committees, who expected to receive considerable compensation from the South London Railway Company as "the railway was to pass through his drawing-room". Roupell added: " Extraordinary statements have been spread about me, such as my having distributed 6,000 cards with the words 'Gin and Water' on them." He finished: "I felt so disgusted with the whole proceeding that I was determined that the fullest enquiry should take place."

The petition, brought by Pattison Nickalls and Robert Bristowe, was dismissed as 'frivolous and vexatious'. (Interestingly, Robert Bristowe was listed in 1860 as living at Dafney House, later known as Daphne Cottage, adjacent to and rented from the Roupells at Aspen House.) Hill suggested that the evidence of at least twelve people, who had listened to the proceedings each day, could have unseated Roupell had they been called to speak. He commented how easy it was to hoodwink a committee of the House of Commons.

A pamphlet published shortly after the election also attacked Roupell. Entitled 'The Rights of Conscience in Danger, A letter to W. R. from a Lambeth elector', it started: 'Your sudden elevation from the obscurity of private life to become the

representative of so important a constituency as Lambeth; the immense majority by
which this borough has chosen you, a man young in years, inexperienced in politics,
and with no known antecedents of public character ... appears to me to merit more
than a passing mention.'

LAMBETH ELECTION

Mr. ROUPELL

Solicits the favour of your

VOTE AND INFLUENCE.

William Roupell's election card

It went on to question how such a large Liberal constituency could ignore Party
criticism of the government system of untried or unproved appointments and replace
a proven representative (Wilkinson) by 'one known only by one in a hundred
electors'. It stated that had Roupell only possessed the legal property qualification and
an income of £300 a year, he would not have succeeded. The writer agreed that
Roupell apparently did nothing illegal and that the system and constituency were at
fault. He wrote, 'The enormous majority by which you were returned to parliament is
the talk in all parts of London; but that which is your *boast* is spoken of as the
borough's *shame*, for they also talk of the enormous outlay by which that majority has
been gained, and they speak of Lambeth as a rotten borough.'

The writer then commented on Roupell's promise to vote in favour of the clergy,
in order to gain their vote. He pointed out that the cries of 'Roupell and No Income
Tax!' and 'Roupell, and the Honour of the British Flag!' were incompatible and that
every citizen should feel a pride in paying his share of the war tax to defend the
Empire. He wondered why Roupell did not try for a larger majority by advocating
'Roupell, and No Tax At All!'.

He then questioned the part played in Roupell's campaign by the popular press in
the shape of the *The Morning Advertiser*. He described the paper as being 'at once the
oracle and supporter of prize-fighting and the true religion, which enjoys at the same
time the special confidence of Heaven and the prize ring'. He wondered how, after
Roupell's allusion to his property in his initial address to the electors, *The Morning
Advertiser* so soon published particulars of that wealth. He contrasted his
extravagance with the thousands of people living and dying in Lambeth in severe
poverty and suffering.

Ignoring such attacks, the victorious Roupell arranged a Lambeth Festival, described as 'The Lambeth Election Fête and Dinner to celebrate the victory of the Electors of Lambeth and Mr Roupell over their accusers.' Reported in detail in *The Times* and the *South London News*, this took place in July in the Surrey Gardens. Five hundred and seventy worthy gentlemen, including the editor of *The Morning Advertiser*, sat down to 'an excellent cold collation', while the band of the Grenadier Guards played and over 4,000 people visited the gardens to be entertained.

Frederick Doulton presided, and among the supporters were Admiral Sir Charles Napier, John Thwaites, Chairman of the Board of Works, W Williams MP and six other Members of Parliament. Other Lambeth notables included John and Henry Doulton, various businessmen and a number of gentlemen who had opposed Roupell at the election. A twenty-one-gun salute was fired, followed by various toasts and speeches in praise of Roupell and 'his great firmness and moral courage'. Roupell gave a long, rather pompous, vote of thanks. The Elliot Brothers, the band of the Scots Fusiliers and Jullien's concerts entertained the visitors in the grounds. The fete concluded shortly after ten o'clock following a fireworks display.

So William Roupell's parliamentary career began. His chambers were near the House at 16 St James's Square. After such a victory it must have been disappointing for his supporters to discover that Roupell rarely spoke in the House. Only one report appeared in *The Times*, quoting his comments regarding the cost of the Victoria Street sewer and the condition of the river Thames. He later justified his lack of participation by likening himself to an apprentice who needs to gain experience; interpreted by some that he took no part in debate because he did not want to make a fool of himself. Instead he concentrated his efforts on the continuing development of Roupell Park and the acquisition of money to fund his ambitions.

Some of the first residents of Roupell Park recorded on the 1851 census included, at Harvey Lodge, Charles Pizzala, a looking-glass manufacturer, his wife, son, housemaid and cook, with a coachman living in a coach-house. Harvey Lodge or Harvey House was later the name given to one of a pair of houses on the same site inhabited by William and Sarah Roupell after their mother's death. An interesting point is that this was the site first mortgaged by William to Louisa Douglas in 1854. The nearby gardener's cottage where William spent his last days was also known as Harvey Lodge, presumably named by him on his removal there after his sister's death. Across the road, at Christ Church parsonage, lived the Rev. Wodehouse Raven, his wife, eight children, six boy scholars in their teens, a cook, two housemaids, a parlourmaid and a nurse.

In June and August of his election year, 1857, articles appeared in *The Building News* outlining Roupell's plans for Roupell Park, at an estimated cost in excess of £100,000. Christchurch and Palace Roads were now laid out as far as the Streatham parish boundary (Hillside Road). Palace Road acquired its name after the new Crystal

Palace, relocated from Hyde Park to Sydenham, which was an impressive sight on the horizon. Christchurch and Palace Roads were to be extended to Norwood Road, along the length of Roupell Park. The area between, in the Streatham half, was to be developed into an ornamental private park with plantations and pleasure grounds for the residents of the large villas, most of which were already built, first along the south side of Palace Road, then along the north side of Christchurch Road. Trinity (now Hillside) Road formed the eastern boundary to the development. Roupell planned to extend Trinity Road to Tulse Hill to meet Trinity Rise. He also had ambitious plans drawn up to build himself a grand house with extensive grounds stretching from Trinity Road almost to Norwood Road, centred on the present Lanercost Road. The Roupell brickfields were sited to the south of this in the loop of what is now Kingsmead Road.

Of these plans, only the extensions to Christchurch and Palace Roads, the planting of trees on the new parkland and the houses were completed. The mainly detached villas were built on the north of Christchurch Road up to the present Fenstanton School, and the south of Palace Road to Hillside Road. Two grand houses, Tower House and Hillside House, stood at either side of the junction of Palace and Hillside Roads (south). The houses in Palace Road, designated a private road with no through access (as now), were particularly grand. The only houses still extant (2001) from the first development are a detached and semi-detached pair on Streatham Hill and two of the smaller dwellings in Palace Road, no. 20 being the oldest.

Roupell's other business activities continued. On 23rd July 1857 he raised a further £12,000 on the Warley land; a week later he sold the lease of the Fore Street pottery to Doulton's. In October he sold land in Lant Street for £2,100 then took out a mortgage of £1,298 on adjacent land. Also in October William was given Trunk Farm, Hants, via a deed of gift from his mother, who stated that it had been her husband's intention to convey it to him in his lifetime. On 7th December he sold the Roupell Street area for £27,586 12s.

On 9th December, in Hastings, his sister Emma died, aged twenty, after being ill for some time. What took her to Hastings, no doubt, was the hope of benefiting from the sea air. Mary

William Roupell MP in 1857
from a photograph by Myall

Haslam (Haslam & Rees, to whom William had been articled?), a widow of Roupell Park, had accompanied her there and was at her bedside when she died. Emma was buried in the family vault on 16th December 1857.

On Friday 25th June 1858, Roupell spoke in the House regarding the cost of the Victoria Street sewer and the condition of the River Thames, both popular concerns. He said that the original contract for the sewer was under £12,000, but it had already cost £73,000 and this could rise to almost £200,000. He criticised the building of so large a sewer, which he considered a failure, and condemned the proposal to build one of similar size on the other side of the river. He endorsed statements as to the effect of the present condition of the Thames on the thousands of people living in its vicinity in a state of chronic cholera, and agreed that if hot weather and warm rain persisted a severe epidemic could result. 1858 was the 'year of the Great Stink' when the Houses of Parliament closed for a time because of the smell from the river.

On 14th July he mortgaged the Hampshire property Trunk Farm for £3,500 and Whitehouse Farm and Gravett Hill for £1,450. In February 1859 the deeds of Glass House Yard, Gravel Lane, Southwark were assigned to him by his mother.

On Tuesday 1st February 1859 at The Horns Tavern, Roupell gave his customary report to his constituents on proceedings during the last session. He was enthusiastically received and his speech evoked three cheers. Doulton gave the vote of thanks.

In April, at the ninth Lambeth election, at which two members were to be returned, Roupell sought to retain his seat. Williams, perhaps sensing some lack of support, announced in *The Times* that he would not stand because of ill-health. Accordingly Frederick Doulton announced his candidacy. However one of his enemies started the rumour that he had bought off Williams, hence Williams reversed his decision. It soon became apparent that Williams had more support than was expected, and Roupell's agents therefore sided with him. Despite the friendship between Doulton and Roupell, the latter declared, at a meeting at The Horns, that he "had the pleasure of announcing that our old friend Mr Williams would again stand for Lambeth". Doulton and his supporters must have been shocked by this statement and, after checking their canvassers' returns, he withdrew from the contest, allowing Roupell and Williams to be returned unopposed.

It was generally considered that Doulton had been very unfairly treated and accordingly a banquet was held in his honour. In his speech Doulton made light of the circumstances of the election, declaring them to be "peculiar in themselves and to the borough of Lambeth", blaming Williams' unfair behaviour and stating that he (Doulton) had withdrawn to prevent a bitter conflict, although he had become increasingly sure that he could have been successful. Neither Roupell nor Williams played a significant part in the coming parliamentary Session. Roupell remained Member for Lambeth until his downfall in 1862, but by now he had found a new role.

WILLIAM ROUPELL
AND THE LAMBETH VOLUNTEERS

1860 - 1862

William Roupell's role as public benefactor now took other directions. He gave a lengthy lecture on the Rev. Sydney Smith to the Walworth Literary Institution. On Wednesday 20th April 1859 at The Horns Tavern he chaired a meeting, as vice-president, of the Surrey Archaeological Society. In June he mortgaged the eighty-nine acres of Bolens Farm, Great Warley to Whittaker for £2,300. Also in June a movement began for the formation of a combined Southwark and Lambeth rifle corps.

After almost forty years of peace and the inevitable run-down of the British Army, the demands of the Crimean and Chinese wars and the Indian mutiny, all between 1854-1860, created nervousness among the people and a demand, fuelled by the press and mass meetings, for a revival of the Volunteers. Recruitment was rapid, members initially providing their own clothing and equipment and therefore being men of means such as middle-class tradesmen, professionals and ex-soldiers. Private coaching and instruction were common; volunteers were both admired and ridiculed.

William Roupell, as others, might have been drawn to support the movement because it provided a position and power he could not otherwise have experienced. In July 1859, at a meeting to set up a Lambeth and Southwark corps, Roupell suggested that Lambeth should separate from Southwark and announced his intention to arm and equip 100 working men. This move would concentrate on the area where he was best known, popularise him to the working man and distance him from the chairman of Southwark magistrates, soon to become the Commanding Officer of the Southwark Rifle Corps. Roupell was largely responsible for raising the Borough of Lambeth Rifle Volunteer Corps.

The following two years were particularly active as Roupell became an increasingly well-known public figure in Lambeth. His was the first name on a list of patrons of the newly formed and lengthily named Brixton Hill, Streatham, Clapham and Balham Amateurs' and

Gardeners' Horticultural and Floricultural Society, which met at the Trinity District school room, Brixton Hill. This was an interest which was to last for the rest of his life. He also maintained his position as MP, if rather an inactive one.

By now Roupell's financial problems were well out of control. To add to these, the country was entering a deflationary period. As the land on which Roupell was borrowing was devaluing, so the interest rates on the loans must have been increasing. Not surprisingly, bankruptcy loomed. Perhaps, an optimist, he had confidence in his property investments. Perhaps he was unaware, or poorly advised, of the seriousness of his financial situation. In August 1859 the Lant Street land was finally sold for the building of a school for the poor of the parish of St George-the-Martyr. In September another mortgage of £6,500 was taken out on Trunk Farm, Hampshire.

1860 was a significant year for the formation of the Lambeth Volunteers and Roupell's role in their development. Money problems did not prevent him from generously funding this new project.

On Monday 16th January, Roupell met his constituents at The Horns Tavern to give account of his stewardship over the past year. He stressed the importance of such meetings and gave a typically vague speech emphasising his support of popular policies and the working class, and his part in the establishment of the Volunteer movement. As usual he was received with enthusiasm and given a vote of confidence.

On 19th January he wrote a Bank of London cheque to pay a debt of £5,000 to the General Life Assurance Company. This was almost certainly the money still owing to Treadwell of Leigham Court at Streatham Hill.

On the evening of 1st February, at The Horns Tavern, was held the first meeting of a committee to form a Volunteer Rifle Corps for the Borough of Lambeth, to be under the command of William Roupell. The nucleus was to be the hundred men whom he had already equipped. He also offered the use of 51 Newington Place and 10 South Place (now 167 Kennington Park Road and 10 Kennington Park Place). The meeting was chaired by Roupell, the resolution moved by W Williams MP and seconded by F Doulton. The hon. secretary was JW Truman, who was employed as an agent on the Roupell Park estate. Subscriptions totalling £134 3s were raised.

Tamplin, in his book *The Lambeth and Southwark Volunteers 1860-1960*, comments that the two years under Roupell's command were years of extreme energy, enthusiasm and activity. He states that there was no doubt that the initial success of the Corps owed much to the drive, personality and money of William Roupell, who laid the foundation on which the Unit was to thrive through many difficulties. Although the large sums of money Roupell was spending were not his to give, it is obvious that they were mainly disbursed on his election campaign, Roupell Park and the Volunteers, and not on gambling and frivolous extravagances as later suggested by the press. His support of the working man, as promised in his election manifesto and at his frequent public parades, also promoted his immense popularity in Lambeth.

Roupell's enthusiastic leadership is evident in the recorded meetings of the Volunteers. A planning meeting was held on 8th February. Six days later on the evening of Tuesday 14th, the first public meeting was held in The Horns Assembly Rooms to form a rifle corps. W Williams MP took the Chair supported by Roupell and addressed, among others, by Doulton. A further sum of £200 in subscriptions was raised. By now Roupell had fully equipped two hundred and forty men and had furnished large drilling rooms and grounds for the whole corps at Kennington, between the premises at Newington and South Places. An enthusiastic meeting ended with the customary three cheers for the Queen.

Building on Roupell Park had almost ceased. Rumours of Roupell's money problems had begun to circulate. On 29th February he mortgaged Bury and Bolens farms, Great Warley, to Whittaker & Woolset for £3,500.

At a meeting held in the Hawkstone Hall, north Lambeth, early in March, Roupell accepted an invitation to become the Commanding Officer of the Corps. On 13th March the Lambeth Rifle Volunteer Corps, or 19th Corps Surrey Rifles, was formed with William Roupell as Major-Commandant. The headquarters were at Kennington. The Corps was now five hundred strong, formed into eight companies, four of which were equipped by Roupell; the 4th Brigade met at Aspen House, where he had created a drilling ground. On 14th June Richard Roupell, aged twenty, and JW Truman were made captains.

*Poster for Public Meeting
at the Horns Tavern on 14 Feb 1860*

On the evening of Saturday 28th June, the inaugural dinner of the Unit was held in the great hall of the Surrey Gardens. Major W Roupell MP presided. Shortly after 7 pm, following a long march through a violent thunderstorm, the soaked Corps arrived at the flag-decked hall for the dinner. Major Roupell proposed the toast to "The Volunteers of Great Britain", and after a short speech the toast was responded to by Lieutenant F Doulton of the Surrey Mounted Rifle Volunteers. A toast to "The Health of the Ladies" was made, then Miss Roupell presented the Corps with a silver bugle from the Ladies of East Surrey. After thanks, Roupell, in the name of the Corps, presented Captain JW Truman, the Acting Adjutant, with a silver salver and a purse containing 100 guineas. The evening ended with the toast-master leading nine hearty cheers for the Major-Commandant.

On July 7th, the *Illustrated London News* reported the laying of the foundation stone of the Lambeth School of Art (extant, St Oswald's Place) at Vauxhall. The stone was laid by the Prince of Wales - his first solo public ceremony. The 19th Surrey Volunteers under Major-Commandant Roupell MP, among many notables, were present. The School of Art, designed by Pearson in a 13th-century style, was said to be an example of funds 'practically applied, not frittered away in useless ornament'.

The first church parade occurred on 5th August when, under Roupell's command, the 250-strong Corps paraded at the headquarters in South Place then, accompanied by the band of the Unit, marched to the church of St Mary, Lambeth. The church was packed with people and hundreds waited outside. After the service the Corps marched back to HQ. On 26th August, amidst large crowds, Roupell marched the Corps from HQ to church parade at St Giles's Church, Camberwell, the new church rebuilt after the old one had burnt down in 1840 (just a year after the marriage there of his parents Richard Palmer Roupell and Sarah). A week later, following the appointment of the Rev. F Statham as honorary chaplain of the Unit, his church, St Peter's, Walworth, became the venue for future church parades.

Also in August, no doubt to Roupell's delight, a sign of official recognition of the Volunteers came in the form of an Order which entitled uniformed Volunteer officers to the same salute as officers of the Regular Army; furthermore, all guards were to pay honours to armed bodies of Volunteers.

Activity continued with the first blank firing on the afternoon of Sunday 8th September on Streatham Common. The Corps (400 strong), accompanied by the band as well as the Drum and Fife Band of the Scots Fusilier Guards, marched through Lambeth to the Common where various drills were performed and several volleys fired. The following Sunday Roupell, presumably on horse-back, led the Corps from HQ through Camberwell, Peckham, New Cross, along the Old Kent Road to the Elephant and Castle and back to HQ. There he reported that arrangements had been made with the 4th Corps (of Brixton Hill) to use their range on Streatham Common for ball practice; also that the large drill ground belonging to the Unit would soon be covered over and lit by gas, thereby allowing winter drill. Practices on the ranges at Streatham took place on Wednesdays and Fridays at 1pm, drill on the lighted grounds on Monday and Thursday evenings and a larger-scale drill, accompanied by the band, on Saturdays.

On Saturday 6th October Roupell led the Corps and Band through Kennington, Brixton, Streatham and Clapham. On Saturday 17th November the whole Corps (650 men) assembled at The Horns Tavern. By now there were nine companies, making it the largest corps in the country. The newly formed Ninth Company, accompanied by the band, marched to the dinner from St Peter's. During the evening toasts were drunk, including to Roupell, and the band played popular airs until the 10 pm finish.

On 26th December officers of the Corps entertained the men to a Boxing-Day dinner at the Crystal Palace; 500 were present. The Corps marched from HQ under Roupell, who presided. The band, with that of the Scots Fusilier Guards, performed. After a speech from Roupell and three cheers for both the Queen and Roupell, the Corps marched back to Kennington.

10 Kennington Park Place used by the 19th Rifle Corps Volunteer Regiment.

It is tempting with hindsight and modern perceptions to smile at the picture of the self-styled Major-Commandant Roupell, playing at soldiers and marching his men through Lambeth in all weathers to the music of the local band and the bagpipes of the Scots Fusiliers, followed by cheering crowds. Neither Roupell, his Captains, nor most of his men had any military experience. His craving for public acclaim had found the ideal vehicle. But Roupell's ability to organise, his charismatic leadership, his energy and enthusiasm are all to be admired. Some at the time must have ridiculed his motives and been suspicious of his vast spending, but he laid the foundations of a successful venture and, in different circumstances and with better guidance, he might have been a creditable member of society.

Roupell's tremendous activity continued throughout 1861, but his business deals were increasingly desperate. A cloud began to gather around him, some of his parasites fell off and he was not seen quite so much in public. However, so coolly did he behave, and so improbable were the rumours of bankruptcy to many, especially his mortgagees, that few suspected the truth. By 1861, the first phase of building at Roupell Park completed, residents included East India merchants, an Australia merchant, a wine merchant, a turkey merchant, several older people of independent means and a bank manager. The Roupells had a maid and a cook living in. His mother Sarah, the head of the household, was listed in the census as a landed proprietor, as was William. His occupation was also given as Major-Commandant of the Surrey Rifles and Richard was listed as a Captain. William's position as MP was not noted, however!

On Monday 28th January 1861, Roupell again gave his annual report to his constituents at a crowded and enthusiastic gathering at The Horns Tavern. His speech opened with comment on the sufferings of the poor during the winter weather and the inequalities of the poor-rates which demanded little from parishes with hardly any resident poor but imposed a heavy burden on parishes such as Lambeth. He commented on the imminent struggle in America but hoped that, whatever the outcome, slavery would be annihilated. He regretted the dependence of English enterprise on the slave states of America for cotton, when it could readily be supplied from India. He called for peace with France and warned Emperor Napoleon that "England Armed is England Respected" and that the Volunteers "with due attention to drill" were effective soldiers.

Questions followed. He was asked when he was 'going to give up the part of dummy in the House of Commons' and when he would 'lift up his voice there against the present extravagant expenditure.' His reply stated that his colleague (Williams) usually spoke for Lambeth, and two Lambeth Members should not speak on the same subject! He said his aim had been to show that a metropolitan Member need not be a noisy Member and that he was prepared to devote his youth to learning. He would not inflict speeches on the House until he had gained experience and mature opinions, and was thus able to express those opinions with credit to himself and advantage to the country. He added that he attended committees and gave real service there. He admitted that there was much yet to be expected of him but, like a factory apprentice, he needed substantial training so as not to repeat the mistakes made by other metropolitan Members whose efforts bore the mark of youth and inexperience. After four years in the House, it is difficult to believe that this excuse was accepted as sensible and honest by his still-cheering supporters.

In an editorial entitled 'If we can't get diamonds, let us wear paste', *The Times* reported the gathering, using Roupell as an example of a number of Members providing fine words and little else: '... Mr Roupell of Lambeth called his constituents together in order to inflict upon them in one dose all that he had through several months mercifully spared the House of Commons. The indulgent assembly, to whom their representative is more endeared by his many kindnesses than by his many speeches, endured the infliction with exemplary politeness. They were, in fact, a little surprised at how very much Mr Roupell knew. He seemed to know something about everything. Why the poor rates would not maintain the indigent, why the affairs of Hungary and Italy were so critical, why we were so disgracefully dependent on the slave trade for cotton, what were the chances of reaction in the matter of reform and church-rates, were all discussed as fluently and confidently as if he had been speaking and writing about them every day of his life. When he had run off these he dallied a little with the Bankruptcy question, threw the French treaty in the air and caught it again, and gracefully passed out with the British Volunteers. The Lambeth people were astonished:

> The more they gazed the more their wonder grew,
> That one small head could carry all he knew.'

'(On being asked) why with such power of speech he was nothing but a dummy in the House ... Mr Roupell remarked ... when he was old and experienced enough he would speak ... Mr Roupell had called his constituents together to tell them he had nothing to say and why he said nothing. This is pushing the comedy of annual explanations a little into the region of farce ... A member calling his constituents together to prove to them his utter inability to speak, and sitting down successful after this proof with three rounds of cheers, ought to be a character with some capabilities, and have a position that something might be made of ... But no-one has ever yet gone so far ... (as to) to make a public apology for never speaking in public ... and give a very sensible speech for never making a speech because he was certain he should make a foolish one ... What human assembly could endure two talking members for Lambeth ... Better far that Lambeth eloquence should find expanse at The Horns, Kennington, than blow up the institutions worthy of reverence.'

Property transactions continued. The ownership and mortgage of the Wandsworth estate was disputed when leases were granted to Henry Muggeridge, the elderly builder with whom Roupell had many dealings. Various transactions in his mother's name occurred over the Thundersley estate.

Interestingly, his mother's address was usually given as Aspen House while Roupell's was always 'Of Roupell Park'.

Roupell presiding at a Banquet

On 28th February 1861 his older brother John, aged thirty-five, died in Port Elizabeth, South Africa, at an hotel belonging to one George Freer in Adderley Street. The death notice was signed by an undertaker and described John as a gentleman with property valued at £10 (probably his clothing and personal effects). A later report in the *Eastern Province Herald and Port Elizabeth Commercial News* mistakenly reported his death as 28th March. His body was brought back for burial in the family vault at West Norwood Cemetery on 12th April.

Roupell was recorded as being absent from parade for a while, being indisposed (presumably dealing with John's death). But by Saturday evening 16th March, he returned to parade the Corps in the new drill shed in South Place, possibly the largest owned by any corps in the country. More than half the cost was met by officers, the remainder by members. Roupell congratulated the members on the acquisition of the drill shed and their improved drill. Tamplin comments that Roupell, having never served in the army himself, showed modesty was not one of his virtues.

He continued his duties of drilling and disciplining the Corps. On 1st April, Easter Monday, along with some 8,000 Volunteers, Roupell and 283 of the Corps participated in a review and 'sham-fight' on the Downs at Brighton. The War Office sent an observer whose subsequent favourable report led to its arranging to mount future such events. On Monday 20th May the Corps dined at the Bridge House Hotel, London Bridge. This was a return dinner for the officers from the non-commissioned officers and men. In his speech the Chairman referred to the "very unusual and continuous acts of liberality to the Corps by Major Roupell", a comment which was received with loud and prolonged cheering.

On 15th June numerous spectators watched the first Brigade drill and parade of the Corps and three other companies at the new ground and rifle range at Peckham Rye. In July the Corps had its first annual inspection at Kennington, took part in a review at Wimbledon, following a shooting meeting inspected by the Duke of Cambridge, drilled at Lambeth Palace and held a shooting match at Peckham Rye, all presided over by Roupell. On Saturday 27th July his younger brother Richard celebrated his twenty-first birthday and coming of age.

In September a Brigade field day was held at Kennington Park and a prize shooting meeting at Peckham. Roupell presented the prizes for the latter: a silver cup and watch, a gold chain and a large number of money prizes provided by the Officers, Members and Ladies of the Borough.

On 16th October Norbiton Park was sold by the mortgagee Louisa Douglas and William Roupell to JG Waite. Enquiries regarding the Thundersley estate continued.

On 26th December the Corps with others marched to Brixton Church where they were joined by the 1st Surrey Light Horse Brigade (Clapham), and the whole parade, under Roupell, marched through Roupell Park to the Crystal Palace for lunch. So 1861 ended on a high note.

Early in 1862 the good life ended. In February, John Treadwell of Leigham Court pressed for payment for land leased to Roupell after his cheque had not been accepted. On Tuesday 3rd February Roupell gave his customary annual address to his constituents at The Horns Tavern. He opened his speech to loud cheers when he stated that he "believed that all would give him credit for an earnest desire to do his duty". He criticised the unsatisfactory way the Bankruptcy Bill had been rushed through committee. Among other comments, he praised the establishment of the Post-Office Savings Banks. He also referred to his early, but ignored, support of the proposal to embank the south side of the Thames. He alluded to the death of the Prince Consort, said he did not think the Confederate States of America would become an independent power; and asked for the continued support of his constituents.

The following day five of the first thirteen officers appointed to the Corps resigned, including Richard Roupell. Three more resigned within weeks.

In March William made an abortive attempt to raise more money as mortgagees threatened foreclosure. On Friday 28th March he told his mother he had "misrepresented the value of the Great Warley estate and borrowed more money than it was worth." Over and above his own mismanagement of his business affairs, Roupell was the victim of the economic slump at this time. The following day, Saturday, he burned a number of forged papers in his Kennington rooms adjacent to the parade ground. The next day he absconded to Spain.

On 7th April, at a meeting in the drill shed, Frederick Doulton announced that Roupell had been compelled to resign for private reasons, and that he hoped the Corps would thrive. Doulton then proposed that, as the Unit had lost a great supporter, a military officer should be invited to take command. It was a year before this took place.

On April 8th Roupell's resignation of his commission in the Volunteers was received and Captain JW Truman (superintendent of the Roupell Park brickfield) assumed command. Much unrest followed, particularly financial. Apparently Roupell had given Truman a receipt for a large amount of money advanced on the furniture and effects at HQ, and most of these had been sold privately, the only thing left being the drill shed over which the bill of sale also extended. All the arms were called in, much to the disgust of the members who had always tried to maintain their reputation as an efficient unit.

Also in April Roupell resigned as MP for Lambeth, to be succeeded at a bye-election on May 5th by Frederick Doulton.

On May 10th only 40 members of the Corps fell in for drill at the Kennington parade ground. By now there were creditors to the sum of £200. On 31st May at parade, it was announced that Captain Truman was to resign and be succeeded by Captain Watkins. It was also stated that rifles would be re-issued. Watkins successfully led the parade for the second annual inspection in July, but he died seven months later.

After a visit by his brother Richard to Spain, William returned to England in August. He attended church in Richmond, where he was recognised, and the following day was arrested in Kingston to give evidence in Guildford of his own fraud and forgery. This was to lead on to his imprisonment.

Hill dismisses Roupell's five years in parliament thus: 'He was introduced to the Queen by a nobleman - became a Major of the 19th Surrey Rifles - and at Christmas time sent handsome donations to the police-court poor boxes'. Comment made at about the time of Roupell's eventual release in 1876 stated: 'William Roupell obtained his seat for Lambeth by the expenditure of £10,000; and if he were released from prison, and would expend another £10,000, he would again be the representative of Lambeth.'

A final comment on Roupell's political career was made in a poem published in *Fun* magazine:

> To Westminster a Member came,
> Of the Liberals a supporter
> And he was returned to Westminster,
> From the other side of the water.
>   (Chorus) With-a-do etc
>
> His father, Dod said, had melted lead
> Somewhere down and about that quarter;
> But the gentlefolks all, they took off their hats
> To the Croesus from over the water.
>
> Now the Lambeth folk this wealthy gent
> As their member did decide on,
> 'Cos they thought he'd set fire to the river Thames,
> What the penny steamers ride on:
>
> But little they knew he'd happen to do
> Some things he didn't oughter;
> For he'd forged a will and several deeds,
> Had this member from over the water.
>
> And the public said, "Well this here Roupell
> Has got no more than he oughter".
> So there was an end of the wealthy gent
> As was member from over the water.

THE TRIALS OF WILLIAM ROUPELL

Guildford - 1862

The litigation involving William Roupell began in Guildford on Monday 18th August 1862. Roupell (Richard) and Others v Waite opened at the Surrey Summer Assizes in a densely crowded courtroom, reflecting the considerable interest which the case attracted from the start. Detailed accounts filled many columns in the press. Books and articles recounted the story, with varying degrees of accuracy, for several years. The Law Report (1862) summarises the proceedings succinctly but the three most useful sources for this history are the *Annual Register*, the Official Report and *The Times*. The Official Report provides a detailed word-for-word account of the entire proceedings. *The Times* also reports in detail, adding comment and readers' letters.

The Great Forgeries of William Roupell, Late MP for Lambeth, Official Report of the Trial at Guildford, in the case of Roupell v Waite from the shorthand notes of Mr G Blagrave Snell, shorthand writer of the Court of Bankruptcy 1862, introduces the case thus: 'The following pages contain the whole of the startling details of one of the most extraordinary series of forgeries that was ever disclosed in a court of justice in this country. No work of fiction, it may be safely said, ever was conceived, in which all the incidents that go to make up a tale of thrilling interest, can be more striking than is this bare, unvarnished tale of truth.

'The principal party concerned in it was but the other day a Member of Parliament, and a man of whom many prophesied that it would be no long time ere he would rise to distinction in the senate; but who, by embarking on a career of reckless profligacy, has brought down absolute ruin upon himself, and upon his family an amount of calamity wholly undeserved, which would have been so far greater had he not voluntarily surrendered to justice by placing himself in the felon's dock.'

The Times introduced the case as 'one of the most remarkable that ever appeared in a court of justice ... uniting in itself a story as striking and incidents as strange as ever have occurred in the most startling fiction ... It is not surprising, therefore, that many persons of the best position in society came to witness the trial, and listened to it with deepest interest.' The trial took place in the Crown Court to allow room for the large audience.

The action was that of ejectment, in which Mr Waite, who had bought the 163-acre Norbiton Farm (or Park) estate, at Kingston, conveyed to him by William Roupell, sought to defend himself against the claim of the heir-at-law, Richard Roupell, the only legitimate son of the late Richard Palmer Roupell. Richard sought to recover the Kingston estate, worth about £15,000, from Waite, who had purchased it in 1861, upon the ground that the deed dated 1855, which conveyed the property to William, was a forgery.

Should the action succeed, so would others involving the Roupell estates, and the unfortunate purchasers would lose their property to Richard. The fact that William would be supporting his brother's action by admitting to his forgeries, and the possibility of him being the main witness for both the prosecution and defence, added astonishment and excitement to the anxiety and interest already present amongst the audience. To quote the *Annual Register*: 'Here was a wronged man pursuing, by the aid of the man who had wronged him, a third man who had never done him any wrong at all. Here was a plaintiff, whose interest it was to show that his own principal witness was a real genuine forger and perjurer. Here was a defendant whose interest it equally was to prove that the man who had unscrupulously defrauded and robbed both him and the plaintiff, was not by any means the scoundrel he described himself to be. And, finally, here was a witness who, of his own free will, quitted a place of security, and came unshrinkingly forward to make statements upon oath, with the full knowledge that the effect of those statements must inevitably be to consign him to a felon's doom!'

The action was tried before Mr Baron Martin. The counsel engaged were among the most eminent at the bar: Mr Serjeant Shee, Mr Lush QC and Mr Browne appeared for the plaintiff, Richard Roupell; while Mr Waite was represented by Mr Bovill, MP QC, Mr Hawkins, QC and Mr Garth. The solicitors employed by Richard Roupell were Messrs J and JH Linklater & Hackwood; those for Mr Waite were Messrs Ford & Lloyd.

Two points of interest apparently not picked up in press reports concern Mr Bovill and Mr Linklater. Some six years earlier, in December 1856, Bovill had represented William Roupell in a civil action, Whittington v. Roupell, the issue being whether a 'small street in Lambeth' (the Roupell Street area) belonged to the plaintiff or the defendant, and if to the former whether a right of way. The defendant in the assertion of both rights had broken down and removed gates and posts erected by the plaintiff. Comment was made in *The Times* report of the voluminous pleadings and the size of counsels' briefs which threatened a case of long duration. However the plaintiff's claim broke down at an early stage and the jury was directed to return verdict for the defendant. The amount of paperwork, the minutiae and the outcome could perhaps be said to be a foretaste of the 1862 action.

Regarding James Harvie Linklater, he was not only Richard Roupell's solicitor, but also his friend and neighbour, living at Boyland's Oak, next to Aspen House. Richard was just twenty-two at the start of the trial. In his will, made fourteen years later, he left most of his estate to the Linklater family who, perhaps not surprisingly, had become a substitute for his own.

William Roupell's fraudulent sale of estates
Illustrated Weekly News 4 Oct 1862

Mr Serjeant Shee, acting for the plaintiff Richard Roupell, and claiming the estate for the legal heir of his father, needed to prove that the deed of July 1855, conveying the property from his father to William, was a forgery. He also needed to prove that the will of his father, dated September 1856, leaving the whole of the estate to his mother, was a forgery; and that both forgeries were by William Roupell. Every effort was made to substantiate these as forgeries before calling William Roupell. Mr Bovill, acting for the defence, considered Mr Waite should not be deprived of an estate which he had bought fairly at a public auction for £7,000 from the mortgagee, to whom it was mortgaged by William Roupell. He used every method possible to make objections to the secondary proofs tendered. His skill and tenacity engaged the court for hours until William Roupell was called.

The proceedings opened with Mr Bovill admitting the heirship of Richard Roupell, thus avoiding the need to call witnesses. Mr Serjeant Shee then recounted the details of Richard Palmer Roupell's family and business. At his death in 1856 his personal property was estimated to be worth £120,000 with about a further £200,000 invested in real estate in Surrey, Essex, Hampshire, London, Southwark and Lambeth. During the last sixteen years of his life these had been the subject of formal disposition by wills, prepared for him by the respectable Messrs Ring, Proctors in Doctors' Commons, whose office was within five minutes walk of his residence. These wills were listed: in March 1839, after the death of his mother Catherine (three years after the death of his father John); codicils in December 1839 and January 1840, after his marriage; a will in October 1840, three months after the birth of his legitimate son Richard, devising the Norbiton Park estate, among other properties, in trust to him; a will in 1843, of which a draft was not kept, and another in 1850 from which his various children benefited but most went to Richard. In 1856, twelve days before his death, he added a codicil leaving various small sums, including £30 to his housekeeper Mrs Hunnan and £150 to two of his executors and trustees, James Surridge and William Clarke. His other executors and trustees were Richard Stevens, his wife Sarah and his son 'called William Roupell', the phrase used to describe an illegitimate child.

Serjeant Shee then described William Roupell's pecuniary difficulties. By 1854 he was in debt to his uncle Watts, the husband of his mother's sister Maria. Roupell therefore conceived a plan to buy land from John Treadwell's Leigham Court estate, adjacent to Roupell Park in Streatham. The sum of £5,000 was agreed. Three years earlier he had led his father, Richard Palmer Roupell, to believe that the Unity Fire Insurance Company had appointed him, an attorney who had recently been articled to Haslam & Rees, as their trustee of a building fund of £50,000, and that they had become lessees of the Roupell Park Estate at a rent of £2,750 per annum, upon which they intended spending £50,000. William told his father that the Unity Company would rent Treadwell's land for £250, thus increasing the total rent to £3,000. So on January 16th 1855 Roupell senior agreed to the purchase and gave his son a cheque deposit for £500 and on the 25th a further cheque for £4,500. William paid the first cheque into Watts's account with the Union Bank and the second into his own account with the Bank of England, forging Treadwell's endorsement signature. After pressure for payment from Treadwell, William agreed to pay on August 1st. To obtain this money, William told his father the Unity Company might lease the Norbiton estate if they were satisfied with the deeds.

Richard Palmer had noted he gave the Norbiton deeds to William to be checked by a solicitor on July 6th. William had them copied by Mr Powell, a law stationer in Parliament Street. He then went with a valuer and West, the bailiff, to value the Norbiton estate, having arranged with his uncle Watts to show the valuers a building scheme to increase the value of the estate to £15,000, so that he could borrow £7,000 on the property to pay Treadwell on August 1st. He then took the original deeds to his solicitor, Whittaker, returning the copies to his father. Whittaker drew up the requested deed of gift on the Norbiton property, William forged his father's signature and took it to Aspen House where, covering his father's supposed signature, he asked two employees, Truman and Dubb, to witness his signature. Whittaker obtained a loan of £7,000 via a client of his, Louisa Douglas. William paid Treadwell and kept £2,000.

In 1856 William similarly had the Great Warley estate deeds copied, increasing the stated rents of the farms considerably to increase the value to £18,000. He had Whittaker prepare a deed of gift on which he forged his father's signature and borrowed £15,000. It was stated that he was apparently unaware of the 1850 will or 1856 codicil.

Then followed an account of his father's death on 12th September 1856. On the arrival of William and his mother at the Cross Street house, the housekeeper, Mrs Hunnum, gave Richard Palmer's keys to his wife, but she, overcome with grief, declined to go up to the bedroom and gave the keys to William. He examined the safe in his father's office then went up to the bedroom and, in a writing desk, found the will of 1850 and the recent codicil. He saw the will left in trust Norbiton Park, Great Warley and Roupell Park to his brother Richard, then a boy of sixteen. To quote Serjeant Shee: 'That will was his ruin - it was destruction to him, to his honour, to his character, to his liberty ... If that will saw the light, he and all who bore the name of Roupell were disgraced ... William Roupell was a bold, able, resolute, determined man - a man possessed of qualities which, if devoted to worthier and higher objects, might have obtained for him an honourable reputation ... So he made up his mind - standing face to face with his dead father on the bed ... A new will revoking it must be prepared, and this time he could not avail himself of the unflinching confidence of Mr Whittaker in his honourable character.'

That night William slept at Cross Street. The following day he visited Muggeridge, his father's eighty-five year old rent collector, at Kennington Cross, on a pretended errand from Mrs Roupell giving him £5 to obtain mourning and requesting a receipt. He then bought a will form, filled it in leaving all the property to his mother, naming her and himself as executors, forged his father's signature and that of Muggeridge from the receipt. He was careful to write with a quill pen, as would his father, apart from his own signature, which was written with his gold pen.

An outline description of Mrs Roupell was then given. She had visited her husband daily during the last week of his life and appeared to know nothing of the will. To quote: 'A woman who has consorted ... for as many as twelve years ... with a man furtively ... never enjoys that confidence which is reposed in a wife ... Little can the woman be the friend, in the full sense of the word, of a man who has dallied with her for years as a toy to be broken and replaced at his caprice - as a woman cannot be what a wife is, the glory of a man, as long as she continues to be his shame.' She was said to have been Richard Palmer's mistress from the age of seventeen. John was born in Clarendon Street, Somers Town; the family then lived in Pitt Street, Peckham, where she was known as Mrs Carter and visited by Richard Palmer on Sunday night. She was described as 'a faithful companion, a true-hearted woman'.

After Richard Palmer Roupell's funeral Watts read the will, dated September 2nd (three days after the codicil to the 1850 will). Surridge and Clarke, the former executors, were not among those present but later accepted William Roupell's explanation and the £150 bequest.

It was then argued that William could not have witnessed a will on September 2nd and therefore it must be a forgery. He was at Roupell Park for most of the day with JW Truman, the superintendent at his brickfields, and had there written a letter to Messrs Barnes, the contractors, giving instructions concerning the laying out of roads on the estate. He had then left for Messrs Gabriel's, the timber merchants of Belvedere Road, Lambeth, to introduce Truman as a customer and write him a reference. He continued to the Unity Bank in the City with Truman, then went to his rooms in St James's Square, then to the nearby bankers Messrs Herries. Truman left shortly after three o'clock. Muggeridge was collecting rents on that day and therefore could not have signed the will.

William Roupell took the will to Messrs Ring to obtain probate but they wanted Mrs Roupell to be present. He later returned with a letter from his mother stating that, as she was so distressed and had such confidence in her son, she wished him to have probate and be sole executor.

William Roupell was then said to have embarked on a career of extravagance and ambition, selling estates with his mother's consent, promising to settle £3,000 a year on her. His brother Richard was described as being a boy who was very fond of carpentry and of horses. He had joined a rifle corps, and had been entered at the Temple to train as a lawyer after school. After he came of age he wrote a letter 'beautifully, distinctly and naturally' to William, dated November 1861, describing his uncertainty as to his future and his wish not to be dependent on him. To the disappointment of the curious, who would have wished members of the Roupell family to be called, Mr Bovill would not accept this as evidence and suggested three-quarters of Serjeant Shee's statement should not be accepted either.

Serjeant Shee stated he would call several witnesses to prove Richard Palmer Roupell died in possession of the estate in question; to prove his marriage to Sarah Roupell and to prove the birth of their son Richard. He would then call Richard and finally William Roupell who, having ruined his mother and his brother, was now ready to do his duty and speak the truth, whatever the consequences to himself.

Witnesses were then called and examined at length. First came James Thomas West of Norbiton Park, who had known Richard Palmer for some twenty-five years and was his bailiff for about six years before his death. He gave evidence as to his ownership of the estate and that after his death he had paid rents to Mrs Roupell at Cross Street until two or three weeks before the sale to Waite when she was ill and had gone to Brighton with her children Richard and Sarah. The second witness was

William Roupell in the dock at Guildford

Mrs Sarah Ann Woods, West's daughter, who had kept accounts for her illiterate father since she was eleven. She said her father usually went to Cross Street to pay the rents every Saturday and that Richard Palmer Roupell visited the Norbiton estate about once a fortnight. Next was Eleanor Wallet who had known Mrs Roupell/Carter for some thirty-four years, having taught the four eldest children in Pitt Street. She was at Aspen House the day Richard was born.

Then Maria Watts, Mrs Roupell's sister, was called. She was the wife of the man to whom William was originally in debt and with whom he was involved in various transactions. An apparently unwilling, muddled or nervous witness, she could not 'remember for the moment' when asked how many children her sister had when living in Pitt Street, as she seldom saw her. She stated she hardly remembered her sister going to live at Aspen House as she was not living near and, as she was on the continent, she did not know when she changed her name to Roupell. She could not remember when she first knew Richard Palmer Roupell, but she knew he had a son John and daughter Sarah; she was uncertain whether Emma was born then. She did not know when he first visited her sister or if he did. She knew her sister had a son and two daughters but she stated 'I never knew whose children they were, it was entirely kept from me'. She was on the continent when Sarah moved to Aspen House and when Richard was born. She now lived in Brompton, having been back from the continent for four or five months. She was accustomed to living on the continent during the season in Wiesbaden, Paris and other fashionable venues.

She claimed she had not seen or spoken to her sister for nearly four years. When asked if there was some difference between them she shrugged her shoulders and made a gesture with her fan. She said she had lived in apartments near Brixton (and Aspen House) for some years but she could not tell how many, giving the reason: 'I have had an accident to my head. Mr Linklater well knows that I have had my head cut open, and I have not a very good recollection. I do not understand why I am thus questioned.'

She agreed with the suggestion that, as Mrs Roupell was in court and well able to state when her children were born, she had been troubled unnecessarily instead of her. She stated William Roupell had visited her at her Clapham home a few days before he went abroad in March, but she had not seen him since and had only that day seen her sister, with Richard and Sarah, at the hotel. She had gone to live near them in Brixton about five months previously, removing on March 24th to Clapham Rise. She agreed she occasionally went to Aspen House during Richard Palmer's lifetime but never saw him there. She said she seldom visited, although she loved the children, but did not want to see Richard Palmer Roupell. On being asked to identify her sister's signature on her marriage certificate, she said her sister was dead (Leah), then agreed it was Sarah's signature.

The next witness William Serle, parish clerk of St Giles's Camberwell, verified the Roupell marriage certificate. William Tarte, lead merchant in Tothill Street, Westminster, a friend and business colleague of both John and Richard Palmer Roupell, asserted that the latter had told him that, because of his father's eccentricity, had he married during his lifetime he would not have been left any property. He also told him that his relations had advised him not to marry the mother of his family but to find someone else. Tarte said he advised Roupell to marry the mother of his children and 'to lose no time about it'.

Jane Woodleigh, employed by Mrs Roupell as a day servant for twenty-three years until recently, said she helped to deliver Richard. She agreed that John was rather wild and that his father had sent him abroad. She stated she saw little of Richard Palmer Roupell but that he was fond of all his children. Mr Lord Huntley, surgeon of Brixton Hill, the Roupell family doctor, attested that he had delivered Richard. He described John as a harum-scarum young man who was wild till he went to school, and then was a little better but was worse when he left school. He understood they were obliged to send him abroad. He described William as a steady young man, more given to learning than John, and thought his father was proud of him. He said Richard Palmer was a good man of business and that, even as an old man, he was still competent and would have been aware that there was £100,000 invested in the Roupell Park building development.

Joseph Sharpe, clerk to Mr George Charles Ring of Doctor's Commons, had known Richard Palmer Roupell for some twenty years through his frequent visits to his office concerning his will. He could not remember the 1850 will but remembered that of 1856, the remaining codicil and the four preceding wills, which were recorded but the copies had since been destroyed.

Then John Treadwell of Streatham was called to give evidence of the sale of his land to the Roupells in August 1854 for £5,000 and the ensuing delay in payment until August 1st 1855, when payment by Whittaker had included £1,000 in Bank of England notes. He stated his supposed signature endorsing Richard Palmer Roupell's cheques was not his. Alexander Balfour, clerk in the Bank of England, was questioned about the cheques. He attested that £500 and £4,500 had been drawn in January 1855 by Richard Palmer Roupell and paid into William Roupell's account. William Albert Clark, clerk at the Union Joint-Stock Bank attested a cheque for £500 was paid in January into the account of Walter Watts.

Finally William Samuel Powell, followed by his father Samuel Goodyear Powell, law stationers in Parliament Street, Westminster, were called regarding the copying of the deeds of the Kingston estate. The son remembered copying deeds onto thirteen skins of parchment but could not remember any conversations, while his father could remember nothing apart from the payment of a conveyance connected with the estate.

At last William Roupell was called. Questioned in great detail, he stood upright and answered firmly and clearly. His addresses were given as Aspen House, Brixton, and chambers in St James's Square. He stated he had been articled to a solicitor, Haslam of Copthall Court, and admitted as an attorney in 1854. He agreed that his elder brother John had gone abroad after a misunderstanding with his father, after which he (William) enjoyed his father's confidence and would see him occasionally in Cross Street and at Aspen House on the weekly visit to the family from Saturday until Monday morning.

He was then questioned in detail on the Treadwell transaction. He admitted forging the deed, naming himself as trustee for the Unity Company, which he showed his father and then burned three years prior to his father's death. He admitted having the Kingston deeds copied by Messrs Powell, then burning these at Aspen House the night before he left England on 30th March last. The deed of gift had been drawn up by his solicitor Whittaker of Lincoln's Inn Fields, his uncle Watts was present at the valuation of the property, the deed was witnessed by his agents Dubb and Truman at Aspen House, and then Watts returned it to Whittaker to raise the loan from Louisa Douglas.

He admitted stealing his father's will, hiding it, then burning it the night before he left England. He said it consisted of a number of sheets, each signed by his father, the executors being himself, Mr Clarke, Mr Surridge of Boylands Oak Farm and Mr Richard Stephens of Tulse Hill. He attested the Kingston property had been left to Richard. He confirmed he forged a new will on a will form; that Muggeridge, whose signature he had obtained to copy, was then an old and infirm man; and that he had first used a quill pen and then his own to show a contrast in the signatures. He had shown the forged will only to his uncle Watts on the morning of his father's funeral. Watts read the will in the presence of Ord, the surgeon, his brother Richard and himself. The will was proved by Mr Ring, his father's proctor then living in Gravesend, after authorisation from his mother. He told of his mother alone visiting her dying husband in Cross Street the eight days prior to his death on 12th September 1856. He said she would arrive at mid-day then he would collect her to take her home at nine or ten o'clock. He agreed his movements with Truman (his building superintendent and military colleague) on 2nd September. He admitted burning papers at Aspen House and the Volunteers' Headquarters on 29th March then fleeing to Spain the following day. He agreed he had committed perjury when applying for probate of his father's will. The case was then adjourned.

The next day four closely worded columns in *The Times* reported events. The *Annual Register* also reported the case in detail. It describes the hush of eager expectation and suspense when William Roupell was called to the witness box. It described him as a gentlemanly-looking man who had to make his way through the crowds. He gave his evidence 'with the most perfect coolness and self-possession, and the most quiet and composed air, though in a tone serious and grave, and as though quite sensible of the effect and the result of what he was saying. Every word he uttered was said with consideration, and sometimes with a long pause, but at the same time with an air of the most entire truthfulness and candour.'

On the second day, Tuesday 19th August, the Court met at 9am The Official Report recorded that long before that time all available seats were filled and the bench was so crowded with ladies that the judge had some difficulty in making his way to his seat. The crowd was not only waiting to watch the cross-examination of William

Roupell, but was also expecting his brother and mother to be called. *The Times* reported that some of the audience had known him since boyhood, some had known him in society and the counsel who was to cross-examine him had sat with him in Parliament.

Proceedings resumed. William Roupell was called. He was described as being paler than the previous day, but retaining his calm demeanour and, despite the long and skilful cross-examination, he confirmed his evidence.

He was questioned first as to the estimated property values from his father's death onwards. The larger estates were dealt with in detail. He attested that Roupell Park, worth £40,000 in 1853, was now worth £200,000 after he had spent £150,000 on it. This was raised by borrowing on mortgage: £70,000 in his father's lifetime and £30,000 since his death to the same mortgagees, and £35,000 to others. He admitted forging the deed giving him the estate, but denied vehemently that in admitting the forgery he was trying to obtain £200,000 for his brother. Roupell Street, valued at £50,000, had been improved by him, but not materially so. He had mortgaged this to raise £30,000 and then another £15,000 jointly with Roupell Park.

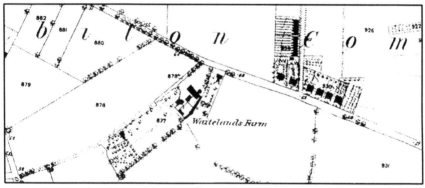

Waitelands Farm on Roupell's Norbiton Park Estate c. 1866/7

Norbiton Park was valued at £15,000, on which he had raised £12,000. The Great Warley estate was valued at £10,000, on which he had raised £12,000, then another £5,000 jointly with other properties as security. Part of this estate he said was legally his from his father. The Thundersley estate was valued at £10,000 in 1855 and £13,500 in 1862, after a portion had been enfranchised the previous year with money provided by Mrs Roupell. The smaller properties were listed along with £2,500 in shares his father held in a number of companies including the Alliance Marine Insurance Company and the Lambeth Waterworks Company. (The latter had bought land from him at Roupell Park for the building of the reservoir now adjacent to Daysbrook Road.) At his death, Richard Palmer Roupell's balance with the Bank of England was £8,000.

William agreed he had received loans upon or sold most of the property. With his mother concurring, he had fraudulently conveyed: Roupell Park, the will to possess this, Norbiton Park, the freehold estate at Great Warley, the lead works in Bear Lane (he seemed unsure whether or not this had been sold by his mother), the Borough hop warehouses, Lant Street (mortgaged and part sold), land in Wandsworth Road, Southville (?) in Lambeth, and a small riverside property sold to Doulton's for £1,000. The total was about ten conveyances. He agreed he had obtained some £300,000 by forgery, to which his brother, sitting nearby, was entitled. He confessed to raising some £77,000 during his father's lifetime on Roupell Park and Norbiton Park, that he had stolen £10,000, this being £5,000 from Treadwell's cheques and £5,000 variously, including Unity Company dealings and rents. He stated he had spent £70,000 before, and £80,000 after, his father's death on building and roads in Roupell Park.

He was then questioned about the forged will. He testified that he had told his mother that his father had made a new will on his advice, leaving everything to her, because in the will of 1850 the phrase, 'my son, called William Roupell', would have revealed his illegitimacy. He alleged it was his father's intention to change the will on August 31st 1856 but, because his old friend the senior proctor was not there, he made only the codicil. A few days before his death, his father, in the presence of himself and his mother, had said, 'I must throw aside all delicacy and do it'. He then took him upstairs, showed him the will and dictated another codicil.

Because of the difficulty in the management of his scattered property, he had decided to secure his wife and children a fixed allowance instead of the property bequeathed to them in the 1850 will. As his father considered that he (William) had proved himself a capable man of business, for example in the case against Whittington, he had decided to leave the whole of the property to him, leaving the rental of Roupell Park, about £3,000, to be divided between the family. But before the details of this could be explained, he had told his father to leave the existing will as he was too weak to continue, it was late, and there were no witnesses available. However he said the true reason for his intervention was because his father had chosen Roupell Park, of which he was wrongly in possession, as security for his family, thus his fraud would be discovered. He said he had seen only parts of the will but he knew of its contents from old Mr Ring's garrulous conversation. He also attested he had always intended destroying the will, without knowing its complete contents, as he was wrongfully in possession of Roupell Park, Kingston and Great Warley. He said he did not expect the will to benefit him but would have been satisfied to retain possession of these three estates and have the remainder of the property go to his brother.

He was then questioned as to his relationship with his father. He agreed he was his father's favourite son, but only for the last three years of his life (after he had committed the 'great fraud'). He denied that his brother John was a vagabond or that he had been sent abroad. He said he had provided John with money to go to the Cape of Good Hope because he and his father had several misunderstandings, because of John's 'reckless folly' towards his father and because his father would not see him and had practically forbidden him to enter his house (Aspen House), refusing to maintain him, although he had no means of support. William stated, "My father was an eccentric man, and although much better than the average of men, he had very little judgement in the management of his children". William denied John had stolen money to give to a woman. He agreed he (William) became the favourite son because he was well behaved. He thought his father was proud of him and expected he might be a great man, although this was never said. He assumed he would inherit Roupell Park, if nothing else, which was partly why he took possession.

He agreed he had exhausted all his resources by March 1862; he had spent his money or been "defrauded and robbed of it". He was asked how much was left of the £300,000, assuming all the deeds and the will were valid and not the forgeries he said they were. He replied that the Essex estates at Havering, Stapleford and Thundersley were left, having been mortgaged by his mother at his request, being worth some £12,000. Also the family settlement of £50,000 on Roupell Park and Roupell Street remained, giving £2,200 per annum before his mother's death and £2,000 after. In addition there was some £10,000 or £11,000 from other sources. However he then said that, because of the validity of the transactions he had undertaken and the outstanding mortgage repayments, there would be very little left of the family settlement. This settlement had been drawn up in October 1860 with his mother, against her inclination, but influenced by his solicitor Rees and by Whittaker, who also wanted Richard's agreement, but William had said this would be impossible as Richard would consult his friend, the solicitor Linklater, who would advise against it. Therefore, should the will be proved a forgery, the settlement would be invalid and the £50,000 would go to Richard.

William was then asked as to the details of the 1850 will. This named William and his mother as executors, witnessed by WR and J Muggeridge, and bequeathed to his mother Aspen House, money and shares, and the early properties in north Lambeth and Southwark, being the factory in Gravel Lane, three houses in Cross Street, rents in Hatfield Place and Cornwall Road, Broadwall copyholds and some ecclesiastical leaseholds. To John was left £200 per annum for life; to Richard: Norbiton Park, Roupell Park, Great Warley and Trunk Farm; and to William: Roupell Street. Copies of both this and the codicil were submitted.

William was asked whether Linklater had ever acted for him. He said that he had consulted him on his brother's behalf in March two or three weeks before he told his mother he had "misrepresented the value of the Great Warley estate and borrowed more money on it than it was worth", and left England.

In conclusion, there being insufficient clear evidence submitted, a settlement was finally agreed. The plaintiff and defendant would divide the value of Norbiton Park Farm and Mr Waite receive a valid title. William Roupell was committed for trial at the Central Criminal Court on the charge of forgery, having admitted that he forged his father's signature on the Norbiton Farm deed and on his will, together with that of John Muggeridge. His signed statement read: "I wish simply to say, I voluntarily left a place of perfect safety in Spain with the intention of returning to England. I returned openly, and was recognised in Richmond Church on Sunday, the 18th inst., and again on the afternoon of the same day on the public promenade between Richmond and Kew Gardens. I do not wish to say anything more, sir."

Comment in the Official Report suggested that the defendant intended to rely on William Roupell's evidence being deliberate perjury to benefit his family and probably ultimately himself. But it seemed the plaintiff had evidence that all statements were true and that the deed of gift of 28th July was a forgery. It was rumoured that an affidavit sworn by Richard Palmer Roupell in September 1855 would verify the Kingston estate was his property, confirmed by an affidavit made by William Roupell on October 2nd 1855. So either the deed of July 1855 was a forgery or William Roupell committed perjury by his affidavit. Also it seemed there was no collusion between William Roupell and his family; that he had determined to surrender to justice under any circumstances before he was aware the present proceedings would be taken.

A number of points of interest can be drawn from the tortuous proceedings. William Roupell's statement that he returned on Sunday, the 18th inst. (did he mean Sunday 17th August?) and the comment above that he was determined to surrender before he was aware proceedings would be taken, do not ring quite true. One sentence in *The Times* report stated the date of the trial had been specially fixed the previous week. William stated he was in Richmond on Sunday and was arrested on Monday, the first day of the trial. It is known that at some point Richard visited him in Spain. It is difficult to believe the timing of his return was not the result of some negotiation.

William Roupell referred to his success in the Whittington case as a reason why his father had confidence in his son's legal ability. The reported civil action Whittington v. Roupell did not occur until three months after his father's death, although, of course, it is possible that there were prior dealings. It is also worth noting he was clever enough to use in his forgeries old and trusted men, who had known and respected his father for many years, and who would not be expected to live to give evidence.

The evidence given by Maria Watts provided a scene worthy of any farce. The idea of her knowing little about her sister's children, marriage or whereabouts, even when she lived near her, again does not ring true. Her apparent avoidance of Richard Palmer, her reference to her dead sister (Leah) when being questioned about Sarah, her fashionable lifestyle, her four-year estrangement from Sarah, her removal from Brixton to the more distant Clapham six days before William went abroad and his subsequent visit to her all provide a tantalising glimpse of an even more fascinating story. Of course the one man who must have known more about William Roupell's affairs than any other was her husband, Walter. It was he who advised the young William and arranged loans, yet he was never called to give evidence. It is tempting to surmise that the marriage between Maria Crane, the carpenter's daughter, and the lawyer Walter Watts, had more to do with the Roupell wealth than her charms, and that the downfall of William Roupell could well, at least in part, be laid at his uncle's door.

The effect of the scandal on Richard, Sarah and their mother must have been enormous. Mrs Roupell, in particular, must have cringed with embarrassment as she sat in court on the first day and listened while her own and William's shame was exposed to all. The account presented of her husband, who had described his father as eccentric and unable to relate to him; then being described in very similar terms himself by his son; the weekend visits, the difficulties and eventual move abroad of her son John, the death of Emma, her relationship with her sister Maria, Richard's love of carpentry like her father, and the rise and fall of her family's place in society: to have had all this rehearsed in public, not sparing details of her marital circumstances, must have been intensely hurtful and distressing. The loyalty of her servants called to give evidence and the obvious determination

THE GREAT FORGERIES

OF

WILLIAM ROUPELL,

LATE M.P. FOR LAMBETH.

OFFICIAL REPORT OF THE TRIAL AT GUILDFORD,

IN THE CASE OF

ROUPELL v. WAITE.

FROM THE SHORTHAND NOTES

OF

MR. G. BLAGRAVE SNELL,

SHORTHAND WRITER TO THE COURT OF BANKRUPTCY.

WITH A PORTRAIT OF WILLIAM ROUPELL.

LONDON:
G. VICKERS, ANGEL COURT, STRAND.
AND ALL BOOKSELLERS.
1862.

Title Page from G. Blagrave Snell's account of Roupell's Guildford trial

of her children to protect her must have been her only consolation. She was not in court on the second day when it was suggested she might be called to give evidence. It was stated that, shortly before the Norbiton Park auction in 1861, being unwell, she, Sarah and Richard had gone to Brighton. Ill educated she may have been, but she had been involved in William's transactions sufficiently to perhaps suspect all was not well. Surely something of the bankruptcy proceedings facing her son must have been apparent to her by the time Norbiton Park was sold. The enormous sum of money her son had apparently squandered must have been incomprehensible to her. £300,000 at today's buying power is in excess of £12 million.

On August 21st *The Times* published a long article on the moral overtones of the case. It commented that the extraordinary case, discussed in all the households of the kingdom, was not only a history of crime, but above all a piece of family history. The error of Richard Palmer Roupell's illicit intimacy with the woman of his choice caused all those evils and misfortunes by which his family has been visited. His subsequent marriage to Sarah was recognised, but the seeds of trouble had then been sown. It went on to suggest that William, even being reckless and extravagant, could not have committed the frauds except for the ambiguous position of members of the family.

Several letters and articles concerning the case were published over the next month before Roupell's appearance at the Central Criminal Court. On August 21st in *The Times* a letter from a solicitor suggested wills should be made before a registrar, thus discouraging forgery and death-bed wills. The following day four letters appeared: one regarding the proving of a will, one from a clerk criticising the tradesman who, in being asked to copy the deeds onto parchment rather than paper, should have suspected something illegal, one from GC Ring denying the possible implication that either his father or his grandfather were aware of the forged will when it was produced for probate and one from 'A Lambethan'.

The 'Lambethan' asked why William Roupell's statement that he had been robbed and defrauded by others had not been questioned. It went on: 'It may be true, and doubtless is, that neither his mother nor brother knew of these forgeries and frauds until the evening prior to his leaving the country, but it is generally believed in this borough that another relative, who has had from Mr Roupell the great bulk of the money he has raised, not only knew of the forgeries prior to his leaving the country, but was cognisant of them soon after they were perpetrated, and has from time to time made this knowledge the means of enforcing his demands.' Was this a direct reference to his uncle Walter Watts?

On August 23rd *The Times* reported that the forged deed of gift and will had been presented to a jury who formally recognised both as true bills, and that William Roupell had been brought from Horsemonger Gaol but, surprisingly, had declined to plead. Therefore a 'Not guilty' plea had been entered.

In the same issue a letter from 'The Tradesman' who had copied the Norbiton deeds stated that as the copies had neither stamp nor seals they could not have been mistaken for the originals. A letter on Tuesday 26th August again questioned why no comment had been made at the trial on the old parchment used for the thirty-eight duplicate deeds of the Roupell property engrossed for William Roupell by a large firm of City stationers. Two days later two further letters of reply on the copying of the deeds appeared from these gentlemen to exonerate 'The Tradesman' from blame.

On the same day a 'Sketch of Mr Roupell' was published in *The Globe*, introduced as being by an observer who used to notice him from the ladies' gallery in the House of Commons. This related that Roupell was well known in the House because, although he represented a large constituency, which from its size was supposed to be free of corruption, he had spent some £9,000 to obtain his seat. The name of Roupell Park conjured up visions of vast wealth and power. When elected, Roupell drove round the Lambeth streets in a carriage with his mother, like a conqueror at the head of his procession. In the House he was no orator or statesman, but he spoke well and with fluency. Readers were reminded that at the enquiry regarding his electioneering expenses Roupell had stated that he would knock down anyone who suggested he had done anything illegal, yet at the same time he was raising money on forged deeds. He was described as being rather short in stature, with an open, ingenuous countenance adorned with a light beard and the appearance of a gentleman.

In *Punch* on August 30th appeared a short article entitled 'Atrocities of the Law' which commented that the moral error Roupell's father made in marrying Sarah too late could, under Scottish law, have been rectified. It concluded that the establishment of this law in England was only prevented by the pig-headed English belief that its law must be right. Yet, it asked, how could this be so in a country where its abstract love of injustice, which had resisted so many reforms, allowed earnings to be taxed at the same rate as interest and a landlord whose rent was unpaid be empowered to seize the goods of his tenant's lodger?

But the most fascinating publication, equal to anything in today's popular press, was a sixteen-page booklet entitled *Life and Confession of William Roupell*. A copy of this is now held in the Harvard Law Library, USA; indeed certain phrases and spellings suggest it could have been written by an American. It was supposedly written by William Roupell in Horsemonger Lane Gaol on Monday September 1st 1862, was published in Shoe Lane (the former home of his grandfather John) and cost one penny. However, because of its dramatic language, its direct quotes from contemporary newspaper reports, notably *The Times*, and its inaccuracies, generally repeated from these reports, it can with certainty be classed as a 'Penny dreadful'. Its fiction was not repeated in the national press.

The cover alludes to every supposed vice, including his reputed marriage, his affection for Mrs K, his love of gambling and the hells he used. It begins: 'Sitting here in the solitude of my cell, stung with remorse at the enormity of the crimes I have committed - without a friend here to console or advise me, and having no communication with the family I have disgraced and ruined, - I, the once-courted and proud senator, that have doomed myself to a life of penal servitude to make reparation to the mother, brother and sisters I have robbed, make this full confession of my infamy.'

There follows a moralising paragraph and a family history. Then, mentioning the friend with money troubles from whom he had borrowed money for books, it goes on, 'I risked my soul to save my friend ... I gave way to the demons Drink and Dissipation'. The money obtained by fraud led him to a higher circle of society. A young girl lived under his protection in a furnished house in St John's Wood, with every luxury. He gambled at cards and on horses, spending his time with depraved men and women. A lurid account of the scene at his father's death-bed follows. Then he met two desperate villains Colonel S---- and Captain C----m who introduced him to further depravities. Another lady was established at Brompton. Splendid dinners were held.

After an account of the election campaign, a harrowing paragraph tells how, while drunk, he confessed his forgeries to the trusted friend from whom he had initially borrowed money, who subsequently blackmailed him, initially with a demand for £5,000. Eventually he gave him sufficient money to persuade him to leave the country. Then follows an account of his life as an MP and with the Volunteers, all the time becoming more ashamed. No mention is made of any property development - or of the marriage and relationship with Mrs K alluded to on the cover. Then comes the confession to his mother, sister and brother of the fraudulent disposal of the Great Warley estate.

Finally: 'I was haunted by the recollection of the pale and ghastly features seen in the house in Cross Street ... I thought of the dear, kind, good, credulous mother I had left at home, in comparative indigence, - of the sisters [there was then only one, since Emma had died in 1857!] whose prospects were once so bright, - of the brother who had looked up to me with so much confidence, yet whose broad acres I had sold...'

Obviously this was a work of fiction, yet it is not unfeasible that some of it was based on rumour which may have substance, such as the possible allusion to Watts's involvement and his being abroad. On 24th September, before he was sentenced, William said he had written an account of his life but had decided not to publicise it because of the damage it would do to others. It seems very likely that the above work of fiction, using Roupell's phrases to add authenticity, originated as a result of this reported account, and not as dated.

On February 13th 1863 JG Waite of Norbiton Park paid £7,500 to the trustees for Richard Roupell, being half the value of the estate. New deeds were drawn up and he renamed his farm 'Waitelands'. He then entered into negotiations to put a railway through his land linking Kingston and the City. This failed so he backed a plan for a Kingston, Tooting and London railway. Before this unsuccessful bill went to Parliament, the unfortunate Mr Waite died on December 16th, just ten months after regaining his farm. Described as a seedsman, his estate was valued at £50,000. Two years later the farm was sold for £29,000.

THE TRIALS OF WILLIAM ROUPELL

The Central Criminal Court - 1862

On Monday 8th September *The Times* reported that Roupell remained in Horsemonger Lane Gaol, unvisited by any member of his family. Normally he would have been moved within a few days to Newgate with other Surrey prisoners but, as there was a detainer for a debt of £600 lodged against him by a lady, it was necessary that an application be made before he could be moved. This was duly granted on September 19th. The report stated the trial was at first fixed for Monday 22nd and then for Wednesday 24th September. It was said that while in Newgate Roupell had not spoken a word in his defence and was very taciturn.

The previous week *The Times* published a law report on a case heard at the Vice-Chancellor's Court on 13th September. Ellice v. Roupell was a bill filed against Richard Roupell, the heir, and Sarah Roupell, the widow, of Richard Palmer Roupell. This concerned the deed of gift of September 1853 of Roupell Park from his parents to William Roupell, who then mortgaged it to the Guardian Fire and Life Assurance Company. The plaintiffs were then in possession of the whole estate except a very small part (Aspen House?), but in April 1862 Richard Roupell prevented them from selling the estate, claiming ownership, contending that the deed was a forgery and either his mother was entitled to the estate if his father's will was proved, or himself, should no will be found. The object of the suit was to examine witnesses who could prove the deed genuine. The examination was agreed, the plaintiffs consenting to pay Richard Roupell's costs. It was also reported that Richard Roupell had similarly taken proceedings against several other purchasers of property from William Roupell, and that the outcome was expected to be as Norbiton Park; the owners paying half the value to Richard, the legal heir.

Attracting intense public interest, the trial of William Roupell at the Central Criminal Court (the Old Bailey) began on Wednesday 24th September 1862. To prevent any future legal difficulties, it was intended to make out a complete case by the production of a number of witnesses to show the signatures were forged, with William

Roupell's statement being confirmatory proof. There had been some surprise on the previous Monday when Roupell again declined to plead, so returning a plea of not guilty; however it was subsequently stated that he had been taken by surprise by the occasion, and intended to plead guilty when he next appeared.

It being understood that the case was deferred until Thursday, there were fewer people than expected in Court. It was held before Mr Justice Byles; Roupell was undefended. The opening statement charged Roupell with the forgeries of a will and a deed, to which he had pleaded not guilty, but now wished to withdraw that plea and enter a plea of guilty. No objection was raised. Roupell then walked firmly to the front of the dock and, after pleading guilty, asked to say a few words before he was sentenced.

William Roupell then made the following speech, quoted in full because it reveals much of his character, his powers of persuasion and his fluency:

" My Lord, I am aware that a British Judge will do his duty uninfluenced or unbiased by either eloquence or professional skill, and my words therefore shall be few and simple. I beg in the first place, to express my regret for any inconvenience that may have been occasioned by the course I pursued on Monday, of declining to plead, and I trust that my solicitor has been enabled to prevent the legal advisors of the Crown from suffering any inconvenience by that proceeding. I did not expect to have been brought up so suddenly. I thought I should not have been required to plead until this morning, and important considerations induced me to refrain from pleading when I was at the bar before the Recorder on Monday. It was my purpose from the first to plead guilty. I never entertained any other intention from the very first moment that I gave myself to justice. I am guilty of these crimes and I confess them, but I must add that my life has been one continued mistake. In my youth I suffered privations of which the public can have no conception. At the age of twenty-one I incurred a debt to purchase books - that debt was contracted with one who was connected with me by the most intimate tie. My friend who lent me money suddenly became involved in grievous pecuniary troubles which caused him to meditate suicide. I could not pay him the money I owed him. I could not get assistance, and I risked my soul to pay my friend. (The prisoner here exhibited slight emotion.) I will not say how that friend requited me. Whatever I have suffered I have deserved. I don't wish to cast blame on any man; the guilt is mine alone, and I admit it is unmitigated guilt. It is true that I have had to bear peculiar trials, but I have not been tempted more than I should have been able to bear, and I repeat that the guilt is mine, and mine alone.

"I wish to cast blame on no-one. I am most desirous to clear everyone connected with me from any share in this most monstrous guilt, and I particularly allude to those professional men who had transactions with me, and who were retained by me to make those deeds. No precaution could have prevented them from being imposed upon by a desperate man such as I was. I grieve that so many innocent persons should have suffered by my proceedings and that they should lose the property which they believed they had legally purchased from me, but the motive for the course I have now taken is simple.

Newgate Prison

"There is no truth in the suggestion that has been made in many quarters that my conduct is to be explained by the fact that being myself irretrievably ruined I have been induced to make these admissions in order simply to benefit my family at the expense of others, without any regard to truth or justice. I submit, my lord, that such a supposition as this carries its own refutation with it. The crimes that I subsequently committed were all the consequences of my first false step. It is true that my father just before he died continued to express the confidence he reposed in me, and he undoubtedly retained that confidence in me after the great fraud that I had already committed. It is also true that he was desirous that I should take possession of the whole of his property, subject to annuities of certain amounts which he desired to be given to different members of the family. But I was prevented by my previous crimes from carrying out his wishes in the way he desired, though when I committed my subsequent crime of forging my father's will I really believed that I was merely carrying out his intentions, and that I was justified in the course I pursued. I do not think so now.

"My ruin has been the result of the course I adopted. I do not say how that ruin has been consummated - it would be too long a story. Since I have been in prison I have written the history of my life at great length; but, upon consideration, I have come to the conclusion that, if published, it would only cause unnecessary pain to others, and would be of no public good. I have, therefore, resolved to suppress this story, and I will content myself by saying that many of the statements made at the trial in Guildford, and the comments that have been made in some of the cheap newspapers, are incorrect, and are only calculated to mislead the public. I am a living paradox; no-one can solve my conduct but myself, and I cannot, therefore, ever hope to be understood by the public. I will, however, say this. I do not argue, I simply state the fact. It is not true that I am personally extravagant; it is not true that I ever gambled, it is not true that I am a libertine. Those who do not wish to believe me will remain unconvinced. To those who love me my statement is unnecessary.

"I will not allude at any length to the terrible events that induced me to leave England, but I will state that when I resolved to take that step I felt that my first duty was not to my family, but to those who had advanced money to me or purchased property of me to a very large amount, believing that I had a legal power to dispose of that property, and confiding in my honour and in my representations. Before I left England I took steps to make the whole of these persons fully acquainted with my guilt, and informed them of all I had done. I told them that I had committed these offences, but they would not adopt any proceedings against me. I remained in England for more that a week after I had made the disclosure, and after I had made a full confession of my guilt, but they did not take any proceedings against me. [Not surprising!]

"During this time I carried my liberty as if it were pinned to my shoulder. I offered to surrender. I had made no provision for myself, and intended to make none, my sole object being to retrieve the past. I pressed them to tell me what they intended to do. In reply they told me that they did not believe a word of my story; that they thought that it had been cleverly constructed for the purpose of benefiting my family, and that if any of my family dared to take any proceedings to disturb them in the possession of the property, they would prosecute them and me also for conspiracy. This prevented me from effecting any compromise, and I found that I had no alternative but to leave the country.

"I did so and quitted England in despair, but it should be remembered that I had ample resources - that I was full of youth, and strength, and the capacity for enjoying life, and that there were many quarters of the world open to me where I could have spent the remainder of my days in perfect safety. Notwithstanding this I resolved to return, and I came back a self-convicted criminal, actuated by sincere repentance for my crimes, the only object I had in view being to serve the interests of justice.

"I know what I have to expect - a terrible fate awaits me - terrible to any man, still more terrible to any man of education and refinement. But if I do possess these qualities I must admit that they only make my guilt the greater. I repeat that I know what I have to expect - and that it is a dreadful fate. I have, however, looked it calmly in the face, and I deliberately prefer penal servitude for life to the existence I had before me - one of continued disgrace, concealment, and passive remorse.

"My Lord, I make no appeal for mercy, I only ask you to believe in my sincere repentance, and my sincere desire that justice, complete justice, shall be done. For mercy I appeal only to that still higher tribunal where alone no appeal for pardon in such a case as mine can duly be made. My Lord, I await my sentence."

Mr Justice Byles, who, it was reported, exhibited considerable emotion, replied that the charges of forging a will and a deed were two of the most serious crimes known to law; far more so than crimes which had previously led to the gallows. He agreed that one mistake from rectitude leads to destruction but he was unable to judge whether this confession was dictated by a sincere repentance. He continued that although in many cases a judge is able to use his discretion as to punishment, in cases such as this no mercy could be shown and he therefore sentenced him to penal servitude for life.

At this Roupell smiled slightly and left the dock. He was removed from Newgate gaol, where the interior had been recently re-built on the single cell system, to the 'model prison' at Pentonville.

The Times on Friday 26th September summarised the general opinion that much of the Roupell story remained untold. While accepting that it seemed harsh to make further comment on a man whose voluntary confession of guilt had led to his downfall, there was much in his statements that remained mysterious and vague. He confessed, repented, yet threw no light on his transactions. On Monday he declined to plead, effectively entering a plea of not guilty; on Wednesday he

Newgate prison cell

pleaded guilty, not because he had changed his mind but because "important considerations" stopped him from a guilty plea on Monday. (Did he think he could influence a jury in his favour?) He entered into a solemn contract of sale with one and gave evidence of forgery to another. The trial was stopped by an agreement between parties, therefore the case was only partly explained.

Was there more to the story? Why should he risk so much because his friend, from whom he had borrowed money to buy books, had money difficulties and threatened suicide? Was this story to give the impression that, in buying books, his thirst for knowledge had led to debt? He said his father trusted him, though others suggest such an astute man of business must have known something of the fraud. He said his father desired him to have the property but this was a contradiction of the previous will. He said it was too long a story to explain and that he had written his story to dispel the lies, implying that there were other reasons for his predicament. He said he confessed his guilt to purchasers but they refused to accept this as they would lose their property, and thus he was prevented from reaching a compromise. This was an inexplicable thing for a lawyer to say. What compromise was possible - unless he hoped to extract money from them to buy their silence. *The Times* finally commented that he deserved his sentence, even though there was some goodness in him and his crimes resulted from one false step. Hints and allusions, common from detected criminals and intended to interest by attracting curiosity, throw as much light on the character of the criminal as the most complete confession.

Comment in the *Illustrated Times* asks whether such an apparently rich cheat, fraud and windbag was therefore unfit to serve in parliament. The writer thought not, as the House of Commons pretended to represent the nation and therefore should represent its follies, vices and crimes! Roupell was the grandson of a lead dealer of whom strange stories were told of his meltings, of his customers and his gains; thus his moral feebleness was inherited from his father and grandfather like gout, scurvy or madness.

Another writer in the same journal conveyed a certain respect and pity for Roupell. He believed the rumour that a relative of Roupell's had blackmailed him, thus explaining the disappearance of such large sums of money. He described Roupell's heavy investment on his brickfield and Roupell Park, but said that the latter, under careful management, was expected to repay some of this. Roupell was described as being short and good-looking, with no trace of guile and having free and easy manners which were dandified but still gentlemanly, well educated and informed, with a talking capability and no signs of fast living.

The writer WM Thackeray, in *The Roundabout Papers*, wrote of Roupell, whom he called Roupilius: 'I have sat near that young man at a public dinner and beheld him in a gilded uniform. But yesterday he lived in splendour, had long hair, a flowing beard, a jewel at his neck, and a smart surtout (frock-coat). So attired he stood but yesterday in court, and today he sits over a bowl of prison cocoa, with a shaved head and in a felon's jerkin. Champagne was the honourable gentleman's drink in the House of Commons dining-room. What uncommonly dry champagne it must have been! When we saw him outwardly happy, how miserable he must have been. When we thought him prosperous, how dismally poor.'

THE TRIALS OF WILLIAM ROUPELL

Chelmsford - 1863

On Tuesday 27th January 1863 *The Times* reported that the convict Roupell, late MP for Lambeth, was employed with other prisoners in picking oakum (loose fibre from old rope) which he did with the same indifference as characterised his conduct while in Newgate. No steps had yet been taken by his brother to dispossess those who held the property under the forged deeds received from the convict, but negotiations had apparently been going on between the solicitors of both parties for some time.

On Tuesday 17th February there was a report that a witness had been found who would swear that he saw Roupell's father sign the deed of gift which the son at the trial swore to be a forgery. It was added that both parties were busy getting up evidence.

On Saturday 28th February, as reported, a further attempt was made by the mortgagees to retain Roupell Park by proving William Roupell's evidence to be lies. This was unsuccessful as proceedings were already instituted and Roupell's confession of guilt made. Four reports of legal points and judgement on this appeared through March, April and early May.

On Monday 13th July it was reported that Richard Roupell was to seek to recover the estates at Great Warley in Essex and Roupell Park in Streatham by disproving the validity of the securities held by the mortgagees. The first case was due to be held in Chelmsford while the second, against the Equitable Insurance Office, was to be heard in Croydon during the second week in August.

Roupell and Others v Haws and Others opened in the Civil Court, Chelmsford, before Mr Baron Channell and a special jury on July 16th 1863. Mr Serjeant Shee, Mr Lush QC, Mr Joseph Browne and Mr Thesiger, instructed by Messrs Linklater, appeared as counsel for Richard Roupell; Mr Bovill QC with Mr Hawkins QC and Mr Garth appeared as counsel for the defendants, the mortgagees. The case lasted eight days. Again a detailed account and many columns in *The Times* recorded the sensational events, eagerly anticipated throughout the country. A book containing over one hundred pages of these columns is held by Lambeth Archives. With over a year for the case to be prepared, it was expected that William Roupell would undergo a far more searching examination than previously in order to prove his avowals of the forgeries a fabrication and that the signatures of now deceased persons on several documents were genuine, whatever mental incapacity or coercion had existed or been used to obtain them.

Richard Roupell claimed the estate both as heir and under the will of 1850. The defendants claimed under the alleged deed of gift to William Roupell and the will of 1856. The original and draft of the 1850 will having being destroyed, and only William Roupell's statement given in evidence as to its contents, it could not be proved that he had not been bequeathed the estate thereby and had disposed of it legally. They claimed he might have forged leases and raised money dishonestly, but the Warley deed of gift of January 9th 1856 and the proved will of September 6th 1856 were valid. If the deed was proved genuine, then Richard Palmer Roupell did not own the property at his death and therefore Richard could not inherit it. Richard Roupell must prove the forgery of the deed, otherwise the mortgagees would gain possession, or the forgery of the will, otherwise his mother would have possession and be entitled to allow William to dispose of it as he wished, Richard having no claim at all.

The large, airy courtroom where the case was to be heard was packed at an early hour, and it was some time before silence could be gained in order to commence the proceedings. A summary of the previous trial, the value of the properties at Richard Palmer Roupell's death, William Roupell's transactions on these and the Roupell history were gone through. Several new facts of interest emerged. Serjeant Shee stated that in 1849 William had been articled to the attorneys Haslam & Rees and was regarded as a wealthy young man. The reality however was different. William was in his father's power. His allowance was only £1 a week. His father was eccentric, very careful with his money and disliked any extravagance or signs of grandeur. He had once flown into a rage when William had been seen riding with a servant in attendance, saying he would disinherit him.

His relationship with his uncle Watts and Whittaker was recounted. Watts, although he was married to Mrs Roupell's sister, did not appear to know her husband, Richard Palmer Roupell. He had been articled to the attorney King, later of the firm Whittaker & King of Gray's Inn. He was very close to William Roupell but from 1845 had lived mainly abroad. By September 1853, William's allowance from his father then being 25 shillings (£1.25) a week, he owed Watts £1,000.

The following month he effected his first forgery, a deed of gift to himself of Roupell Park, on which, in November and December, Whittaker, acting as William's attorney, advanced two loans each of £1,000. These were repaid in January 1854, out of £10,000 which Whittaker got a client of his, Miss Douglas, to invest in Roupell

Park. In July 1854 Richard Palmer Roupell gave notice to the tenants of Roupell Park to pay their rents to William. Although acting otherwise and advancing large sums of money on the estates over the following months on security of the property, William still appeared to be under the control of his father. The advances were made through Whittaker, via Watts, then by clients of Whittaker. At no time did anyone refer to Richard Palmer Roupell regarding the deeds of gift involved.

In January 1856 William qualified as an attorney but by then he owed Whittaker £2,500. He had three bankers: the bank of England, Herries & Co, to whom he owed £9,500, and the Unity Bank. He owed the London and Westminster Bank, as guarantor of Whittaker, £12,000 due in February. Thus the deed of gift on the Warley estate was forged.

The estate consisted of two farms at Great Warley: Bury, 250 acres, leased to Messrs Haws at a rent of £250 a year, for twenty-one years from September 29th 1842, and Bolen's or Bullen's, seventy acres, forty freehold and thirty copyhold, which latter part Richard Palmer Roupell had conveyed to William to enfranchise in 1855; the whole being leased to a tenant called Springham at a rent of £78 a year. The deed of gift was via a letter, purporting to have been

Chelmsford Assizes

written by Richard Palmer Roupell, but actually written by his daughter Sarah at Aspen House on January 8th 1856, with her father's signature forged by William. He also forged the leases to enhance the value of the property. An attempt to mortgage it to a Mr Longman failed because the latter's legal adviser questioned Richard Palmer Roupell's lack of involvement. The property was then mortgaged to the real defendants, Messrs Freeman, for £12,000, including the forged leases giving the rents as £560 and £178, rather than £250 and £78. The 1856 proved will of Richard Palmer Roupell, in William's handwriting and which he said was forged, was quoted.

After the lunch break the first of what was expected to be a large number of witnesses was called. This was the most unimpressive Maria Watts, Mrs Roupell's sister. She stated that Richard had been born in 1840. She had not been present at her sister's marriage and had not seen her since the Guildford trial the previous summer. She lived at Brompton. She denied she went to Baden-Baden (where her husband was supposed to live), but admitted she sometimes went to Wiesbaden. She then became very excited and said she was a poor, friendless, penniless woman. Being pressed as to whether she was expecting to receive money from other quarters, she said she hoped to be able to obtain funds from the property of which she had been deprived by William Roupell. She said she had been promised this by the plaintiff's solicitors. Being pressed as to this a good deal, she became hysterical, so much so that the Judge frequently had to intervene.

She agreed she knew William Roupell well. After a great deal of difficulty as to her understanding the question, she denied saying the property had been left to her sister to avoid the 10% inheritance tax. She said John had been sent abroad to give him a chance to be reclaimed and that his father had given him an allowance of some £200 per annum. She stated she was proud to know William Roupell, in spite of all his misfortunes. At the suggestion that the solicitors would intercede for her should William succeed in getting back the property, she became very excited, incoherent and unintelligible. She said everyone who knew her nephew was proud of him; she thought his father had been also and that he had said his son would be a great man one day; which he was. She said she knew nothing about Richard Palmer Roupell and disliked him. She then stated she had been deserted by her husband and that she had never visited the old man (Richard Palmer Roupell). On re-examination she said she had mortgaged a house of hers to William Roupell and it was concerning this that the attorneys had promised to intercede as it could be lost because William was a convict with no legal rights. She then proved her sister's handwriting.

Four more witnesses were called. The elderly Jane Woodleigh remembered Richard's birth in 1840 and the ages of the other children. William Tarte repeated his Guildford statement when he advised Richard Palmer to marry Sarah. He said Gravel Lane was a very low neighbourhood and laughed at the suggestion that lead-smelters John and Richard Palmer Roupell would melt anything. He stated that the latter was a man of a few words who did not get on well with his son John ("He could not get that boy up in the morning"), but seemed fond of William. Two female witnesses attested they had lived next door to Sarah, known as Mrs Carter, at Pitt Street, Peckham, and had seen Richard Palmer leave the house in the morning. They thought he was Mr Carter but had never spoken to him.

William Roupell was then called. He was described as being not in convict dress but so altered as to be unrecognisable. He answered questions quietly and coolly. He agreed his mother had lived at Pitt Street where she was known as Mrs Carter. He had no knowledge of his parents' marriage at the time, but his mother was known as Mrs Roupell after her removal to Aspen House in 1839. He never heard his father mention her maiden name. He described his father's visits to Aspen House; at first twice a week and then once, from Saturday to Monday morning when he returned to Cross Street. He described his father as being careful and inexpensive in his habits. He recounted that he had been articled to Haslam and his successor Rees, slept at Aspen House, and had an allowance, first of £1 a week, then twenty-five shillings until his father's death, which had led to his money difficulties.

He then described in detail the Great Warley transactions. He said his father had told him he had transferred to his name the copyhold portion of the estate for enfranchisement in July 1855. At Cross Street, he asked his father for the title deeds for enfranchisement and his father had gone to his iron safe and, being unable to distinguish between the copyhold and freehold deeds, given them all to him. William said he had recorded the receipt but had confused the location with the nearby Havering property, which his father corrected. The receipt book with this alteration was shown, to prove how carefully his father checked every business transaction. He took two of the deeds, the leases to the tenants of the farm, which he had copied by Messrs Waterlow, the law stationers, in order to alter the rentals. These with his father's forged signature were witnessed by Truman and Dove, who thought they were witnessing his (William's) signature. The copies, along with the deeds to the property, he gave to Whittaker in order to convey it by deed of gift to himself via the letter dictated by him to his sister Sarah. He hid the original leases in his bureau. He admitted to the forgery and that he had told Whittaker to raise as much money as possible on the property. A long discussion ensued in the court room when both sides argued over points of law, both leases were separately produced and each tried to force the other to call Whittaker. The case was then adjourned.

On the second day the examination of William Roupell on the forged leases continued. He said he did not know where the altered copies of the leases were; he thought he had destroyed them. He stated that after they had been copied he had altered the date, inserted his own name instead of his father's as lessor, altered the terms and rental, then had them recopied and given to Whittaker for the unsuccessful attempt to raise £6,000 from Mr Longman. He said he had forged Haws's signature, which was witnessed by Truman, who trusted him, after he had confused him by mixing up papers. In a letter from Roupell to Whittaker dated September 2nd 1856, regarding the subsequent mortgage of £12,000, mention is made of Watts's imminent return home. Roupell said he had burnt his copies of the forged leases the day before he left for Spain. He had forged Springham's signature and invented the witness Goddard, farmer of Warley.

Hours of obstructing objections followed. Roupell, when questioned about the witnesses to the deed of gift, said Truman was a superintendent of his brickfield on Roupell Park and Dove his land agent there. The genuine counterparts of the leases taken from his father's box he had given to Whittaker's brother and partner, before he left England. Whittaker, however, had been unaware of them until Roupell's confession to him on March 18th 1862 before he fled the country.

Responding to further questions, Roupell declared that he was unaware of the codicil to the 1850 will until his father showed it to him two days before his death on September 12th 1856. He said his father had told him that Roupell Park needed great skill in management and that the property should be left to all his remaining family who would receive an income from the £3,350 a year rent he thought was being paid by the Unity Company. He did not want to leave the estate to his wife as he did not want to expose her to the offers of marriage from fortune hunters which could ensue. William told how he persuaded his father to leave the will unaltered, and that he did not read the will at that time.

Then followed the account of the death-bed scene when William said he removed the will from his father's bureau and put it in his portable writing-desk, carrying it around for about a week before he read it. He said he had been carrying the writing desk around with him for about a year. It was about sixteen inches by twelve in size and contained his cheque book and a few letters. On reading the will he saw that the Warley estate, subject of his recent forgeries, had been left to his brother. He therefore destroyed it and forged a new one. He agreed he had committed perjury over the will, had cheated his clients out of £12,000, and had sold some of his mother's shares and kept the proceeds. He denied he was constantly in communication with Messrs Linklater, his brother's attorneys.

JW Truman and J Dove were called to identify their own signatures and William Roupell's writing and signature. Truman attested he had been frequently in Roupell's company for some years and confirmed his movements on September 2nd, the date of the forged will. He affirmed Roupell had written a letter of complaint to a contractor between 10 and 11am, gone home at 1pm, then had driven with him in a phaeton to Messrs Gabriel's, the timber merchants, at Lambeth, then to the City, then to his chambers in St James's Square at 3.30 or 4pm, where he left him. He said he had visited Roupell in his private room in a house in Kennington in March 1862, the day before he left England, and could smell burning through the half-open door when an irritated Roupell answered his knock. The next day, after Roupell's departure, he saw ashes of burnt papers. Under cross-examination he said that although the brickfields were called Truman and Company, he was only an agent and the owner was Roupell. He was paid £300 a year plus commission on any building work he superintended. He thought his name was used because of Roupell becoming an MP; he now regretted this. He had started working for Roupell in 1854 and trusted him. (He had been a captain with Roupell's Volunteers.) He was no longer a builder, he was a publican.

The object of this examination was to elicit that the signature of Richard Palmer Roupell was already on the deed when they signed, and that the story that William Roupell had led them to believe that they were witnessing his signature only was untrue. Truman said he had seen William sign a deed, he trusted him when asked to sign things and that he had never seen Richard Palmer Roupell's signature. Similarly, the next witness Joseph Dove also said he had trusted Roupell and that he had been called back to witness Roupell's signature after settling the weekly accounts at Aspen House. He said he assumed Roupell was writing his signature and nothing else but that he could not see because he was writing very quickly. He also denied ever seeing Richard Palmer Roupell's signature. During the long cross-examinations of Truman and Dove, William Roupell remained standing. The case was adjourned at 5 o'clock.

Comment was made in *The Times* on Mr Bovill's prolonged and severe cross-examination of Truman and Dove, the two witnesses of the deed of gift. It had been very difficult to follow because deed after deed, the false leases as well as the deed of gift, had been shown to them without identification in order to test their memory or credibility. In declining to cross-examine William Roupell, except to make him repeat the list of his alleged frauds and lies, Mr Bovill made it plain that he intended to contend that the witness could not be believed and that the story of his forgery of the deed of gift was concocted when the forgery of the leases was about to be discovered.

Roupell in his prison cell - Illustrated Weekly News 4 Oct 1862

The first witness called on the third day was Henry Muggeridge, the son of old Muggeridge (deceased), the witness to the forged will, both rent collectors for the Roupells. He was also questioned at length with every minute point being contested. One interesting exchange between Mr Serjeant Shee and Mr Bovill concerned a photograph of the supposed forged will when Muggeridge was asked to identify his father's signature and seemed unsure about it. Serjeant Shee refused to accept that a photograph was writing and therefore could not be used for the purpose of comparing signatures. Bovill said it was a new art which was a method of reproduction of the handwriting. The Judge expressed grave doubts so this and the previous document, also a photograph, were withdrawn. Muggeridge was again asked to confirm his father's signature on documents but was unsure.

Questioned as to the interest he received on his investments in the Roupell property he stated he paid about £400 a year for the Wandsworth land, receiving £600 in rent; £120 for Lant Street land, receiving £50; and had invested £50,000, which he borrowed, in Roupell Park. He denied being promised the title deed should the Roupells regain it.

Mr Longman, the solicitor who in 1856 had advanced the £6,000 loan to Roupell via Whittaker, was then called. He testified that on being asked to advance a further mortgage he had been advised to refuse unless Richard Palmer Roupell was involved. As this was not conceded, he demanded and received the repayment of the original £6,000.

The two tenants of the Warley estate then gave evidence. Springham, the tenant of Bolens Farm rented for £80 a year, said Richard Palmer Roupell visited the farm two or three times annually and that the rent had been paid in Cross Street until his death, then to young Muggeridge for William Roupell, his father's executor. The last rent to Cross Street had been paid in July 1856 (six months after the supposed deed of gift of the estate to William Roupell). He remembered the estate valuers coming, but they did not question him. He agreed Richard Palmer had once said William Roupell was to be the Warley landlord. After his lease had expired in 1862, there had been an agreement with the mortgagee's agents to rent at £100, and when he was later sued for possession he had gone to Roupell's attorneys who had agreed to defend him on behalf of the Roupell family. Similar evidence was given by Haws, the other tenant, who also showed Richard Palmer Roupell had been the owner and manager of the estate until his death.

Several more witnesses were called. Mr Sharpe, employed for thirty years by Messrs Ring, remembered the 1850 will but thought the draft had been destroyed after the 1856 will had been proved. He remembered the 1856 codicil being drawn up. Mr Ring gave similar evidence. Mr J Surridge, who had rented a farm from Richard Palmer Roupell and knew him well, identified his handwriting. He said he had last seen him with Mrs Roupell when he dined with them in Cross Street on September 1st 1856 (the forged will was dated the next day), and had been told he was the executor named in the 1850 will. He confirmed he had received the legacy of £150 from that will.

Mrs Hunnum, the Cross Street housekeeper, said Richard Palmer Roupell slept at Cross Street except on Saturday and Sunday nights. She described his illness and death. William Roupell came to the house at 8am on the day of his death, slept there until the funeral, then afterwards came frequently. She saw him writing letters before the funeral and knew there were papers in the bureau. Muggeridge had not visited the house after the dinner on September 1st, therefore he could not have witnessed the will there the following day.

William Roupell was then called to confirm the codicil legacies he had paid to Surridge, Clarke, Mrs Hunnum and others. He confirmed his movements with Truman on September 2nd and swore that he did not see Muggeridge. Mrs Hunnum was questioned about his writing case which she said she had never seen him carrying, although she had seen it in his brougham (carriage). Witnesses were called to attest William Roupell's visits on September 2nd and Thompson, a clerk for thirty years at Glynn's Bank and a tenant of Richard Palmer Roupell, was called to agree the will of 1856 was not in Richard Palmer Roupell's handwriting; the signature, he thought could have been traced. The case was then adjourned.

On the fourth day, after Thompson had been cross-examined as to his opinions and experience of handwriting and forgeries, old Muggeridge's grandson and widow were called. The grandson described how, as a boy of thirteen in 1856, he would accompany his grandfather, who was over eighty, as he collected Roupell's rents. They normally left the house between 11am and mid-day and returned by 4pm. They collected on Mondays, sometimes other days, and accounted on Fridays. They collected at Wandsworth and, usually on a Tuesday, at Lant Street. On Friday they waited in an outer room at Cross Street while the rents were paid in. September 2nd was a Tuesday so Muggeridge could not have attested a will at Cross Street. Mrs Muggeridge said her husband had died in February 1857, aged 85. She often accompanied him to collect rents, and always to Lant Street which he did not like visiting alone. (Perhaps because of its proximity to the debtors' prison, the Marshalsea. In *Pickwick Papers*, Dickens describes Lant Street as being a melancholy place on rent-day, with a migratory population usually disappearing the previous night.) She was shown a number of documents covered with paper with apertures cut to show only her husband's signature, but she was unsure as to which were genuine.

Various clerks, tenants and business associates of Richard Palmer Roupell were then called to confirm points already given in evidence regarding his signature and careful business habits. Three well-known expert lithographers, Messrs Netherclift, Chabot and Matheson, all agreed that Richard Palmer Roupell's signature and others on the deed, letter and the proved will were forgeries and had been written by William Roupell. Netherclift said that he was frequently consulted as to forgeries and had been consulted by Messrs Linklater four months before the 1862 trial (the month Roupell absconded to Spain).

Finally Caldwell, a female servant at Aspen House for seven years - from three years before Richard Palmer's death, attested that William Roupell slept at Aspen House, took his writing desk out on business and kept it upstairs. A flyman said he had driven Roupell, with the writing desk, from Cross Street every day for a week after his father's death. The plaintiff's evidence was thus completed without calling as witness either his sister Sarah, or Whittaker.

Sarah Roupell *was* called, however, on the fifth day, as first witness for the defence. As she was called, William Roupell, who had been sitting at the back of the court, suddenly said he felt faint and wished to leave the room. He was taken out and did not return until her examination ended. She testified writing the letter of January 8th 1856 supposedly giving the Warley estate to William. She denied knowing anything about her mother acknowledging a deed giving Roupell Park to another son. She stated she and her mother had been staying in apartments in the town but had not been present in court. She denied that the current proceedings were against the wishes of her mother and Richard but said that he would have taken any other means possible in order to avoid further exposure of his family. She identified the letter which she had written at Aspen House at William's dictation as he stood beside her. She also agreed she had written, on her mother's behalf, the letter requesting that William should prove the will of 1856. She said she sometimes wrote and signed her mother's letters to save her the trouble.

Mr Bovill then addressed the jury in a speech lasting over four hours. He asked why Sarah, Whittaker and Mrs Roupell had not been called to give evidence for Richard Roupell, suggesting there might be some family secret they might reveal. He pointed out Sarah had testified she had written the letter at William's dictation, whereas he said she copied his draft. He alleged the Roupell family were making a desperate attempt to regain estates worth £200,000 and that their story was complete fabrication. The idea that William was only a clerk with an allowance of 25 shillings a week when the supposed forgeries began, was ridiculous. In fact, since 1853 he had been in the confidence of his father, managed estates, developed the estates, employed a building manager, had various bank accounts and was dealing in thousands and borrowing tens of thousands. There were contradictions in evidence over the timing of the 1856 deed. He suggested Roupell forged the deeds only because the forgery of the leases, to raise more money for himself, was discovered, and that he already owned the property. Comment on the wills followed. He asked why Roupell had carried the 1850 will around in his writing desk then destroyed it at the time it would have been most useful to Richard, had it said what he testified. Mr Bovill alleged that Richard Palmer Roupell gave the Great Warley farms to William at the same time he was supposed to have willed them to Richard and that the 1856 will was genuine, giving the properties to his widow in order to save succession duty.

At three o'clock further witnesses were called to identify signatures, including the secretary of Lambeth Waterworks Company, in which Richard Palmer Roupell had shares. *The Times* commented that each of these witnesses produced a bundle of old Roupell's receipts, adding to the mass of genuine documents to be submitted to the jury to compare handwriting.

The sixth day produced a long succession of tenants, bank employees and other witnesses to attest Richard Palmer Roupell's signature. Mr Clarke, a rent-collector and broker for Roupell, said he went to the factory almost daily and had been told by

Roupell in July 1856 that he was an executor of the 1850 will and the codicil of August 30th 1856. He said he had seen old Roupell before his death and was sent for on his death, whereupon he sent for William and his mother. He stated William had slept at Cross Street after the death, in the parlour as the house had only two bedrooms and his father was in one. He said William Roupell had paid him the £150 legacy. He had accepted the will of September 2nd 1856 as genuine, but agreed he had later said it was a good imitation, then again had said it was genuine. He had told the plaintiff's attorneys that he now thought the will was not genuine. They then asked him to renounce his trusteeship, the £150 being guaranteed by them, but he was advised not to do so.

William Roupell

Edwin Whittaker, attorney and brother of Edward, William's attorney, said he saw William sign the deed of gift, that the witnesses' signatures were already in place, that the deed had been accepted before February 11th and sent to Richard Palmer Roupell for execution. He said he and his brother had been introduced to William Roupell by Watts. He knew that Watts had been abroad some years before 1853 and had heard that this was because he had money difficulties. He knew his brother had raised money on securities for Roupell but said he did not know whether any money was raised for Watts. The signatures were again examined.

After further witnesses were questioned as to the enfranchised part of the estate, Mr Bovill gave a lengthy summing-up regarding the handwriting and signatures. *The Times* commented that during the whole of this speech William Roupell came forward to listen with evident interest to an argument directed to show that he had not committed the forgery to which he had sworn.

Mr Bovill continued his address on the seventh day. He outlined the various contradictions in Truman's and Dove's evidence as to the timing and signatures on the deed of gift of the estate in question. He alleged the prosecution dare not call Whittaker because his evidence would conflict with Roupell's. He alleged the witnesses had been influenced by the story of the forgery circulated in pamphlets around the country; that the evidence was unsound; Roupell was not to be trusted and had been proved an inexpert forger; and that family members and friends had not been called because they would have said the deed was genuine.

Bovill stated the story of the will of September 1856 was irrelevant to this case and that the letter supposedly written by Sarah on January 8th was suspect. He drew attention to William Roupell who had been allowed to sit throughout the proceedings, sending notes to his brother's solicitors to assist them to carry out his fraud. He suggested that Roupell being taken ill and carried out of court as his sister was called implied the two shared a guilty secret; perhaps the letter was not genuine or had not been written when dated.

He alleged Roupell's story of the will was inconsistent. He questioned why Roupell hadn't agreed to his father's supposed wish to make a new will, in his favour, just before his death. He again asked why the 1850 will should be carried around for six years then destroyed by him just when it would have been of use to his brother. He alleged that either the 1856 will was genuine and had been made to avoid succession duty or that the 1850 will had given William Roupell the property and therefore its sale was legal. He alleged that he forged the leases and when this was discovered he then admitted to the forgery of the deed as he could suffer no further penalty. This forgery had not been proved, therefore the deed was genuine. At 1 o'clock, after speaking for three hours, Mr Bovill concluded.

Speaking for the plaintiff, Serjeant Shee said that as the deed of 1856 was forged and the destroyed will of 1850 could not show William Roupell had been left the Warley estate, then Richard Roupell was the legal heir. He spoke of William Roupell's repentance and wretchedness. A loud burst of applause followed his statement that the case did not rest only on the testimony of the poor unhappy Roupell.

He alleged that there was no proof that Richard Palmer Roupell had ever given anything to anyone, apart from surrendering the copyhold part to William to save on enfranchisement, but this gave him no right to the whole estate. Roupell had confirmed the 1850 will gave the Warley estate to Richard. If the deed was genuine it would have been more advantageous to Roupell to admit the truth about the forged leases to Whittaker and sell the property to pay off the mortgagees, rather than admitting to a forgery he hadn't committed to escape the penalty of the one he had. All the attesting witnesses were respectable and had confidence in William Roupell. Their evidence about the times was confused because of the number of deeds they dealt with for him. Truman had great confidence in Roupell and would sign anything he asked, but he did not know one deed from another.

His comment that Bovill had tried to frighten Sarah out of her wits, although he was usually so polite to ladies, brought laughter in court. He said her letter could not have been written with their father's knowledge because it mistakenly referred to the estate being at Havering, a mistake corrected elsewhere by Richard Palmer Roupell. The latter was a very careful businessman who wrote everything himself. Serjeant Shee said he had tried to spare Sarah the ordeal of being called. He said Whittaker had not been called by Bovill because it was not in his interests to do so. Instead he called his brother who knew nothing about the deed. Whittaker knew all about Roupell's transactions, he knew the letter had been written by Sarah on the stated date. The young Roupell had fallen into the hands of Watts, who had introduced him to Whittaker. Watts, via Whittaker, had plundered and betrayed the doomed and miserable Roupell whom he described as an object of compassion who, without a satisfactory paternal example, had fallen into the hands of Watts.

He averred that William Roupell had destroyed the will because, after his father's death, he read Warley had been left to Richard, thus his fraud with the leases would have been discovered. Already in serious money difficulties, he devised a will leaving everything to his mother so only one witness, who was very old, would be needed. With the help of Watts and Whittaker, he soon sold the property. On Bovill interrupting him, Serjeant Shee caused laughter by objecting and commenting on the length of time he had already spoken. The case was adjourned.

On the eighth and final day of the prolonged proceedings, Mr Baron Channell summed up the evidence. He exonerated Sarah Roupell from blame. The foreman of the jury asked if they could refer to the accurate reports in *The Times* to aid their memories but he was told to refer to the shorthand notes. The judge said unsubstantiated evidence given by William Roupell must be regarded as suspect and left them with four questions: Was the deed of gift signed by old Roupell in the presence of the two witnesses? If it was not so, was it actually signed and sealed by him, whether or not in the presence of the witnesses? Was the will of the 2nd September 1856 genuine? If not, did the will of 1850 leave the estate to Richard Roupell? The foreman of the jury asked if there was any evidence that William Roupell was in the habit of preparing deeds for his father. The judge did not know of any and suggested the evidence implied not, as Richard Palmer Roupell read everything he signed.

The jury retired at 2.55pm. *The Times* commented that the shorthand notes formed a pile about a foot in height and would overwhelm the jury who would probably be totally confused anyway. The jury returned at 6pm. They agreed that the deed was not signed by Richard Palmer Roupell in the presence of two witnesses. It would still be valid without being witnessed, however they could not agree whether Richard Palmer Roupell had signed it. They agreed the will of September 2nd 1856 was not his and was therefore a forgery, but they considered William Roupell's evidence as to the 1850 will insufficient to determine to whom the estate had been left. The jury then retired again until 7.30pm when they stated there was no prospect of further agreement. The judge then made an alteration to the fourth question: did the will of 1850 devise the estate to anyone else other than Richard Roupell? William Roupell had remained in court awaiting a verdict for nearly eight hours. During the long discussions he came forward from the back of the court and watched everything anxiously, as of course did the other interested parties.

The Times could not report the conclusion of the trial until the next day as the last train for their reporter left Chelmsford at 9 o'clock. The jury still could not agree whether or not the deed of gift had been executed by Richard Palmer Roupell. The judge directed that, if in doubt, the jury should give a general verdict in Richard Roupell's favour because of the enormous expense of a new trial. They again retired at 10 pm but could not reach a verdict. At 10.30pm, after the judge had conferred with both sides, the jury was discharged.

At the opening of the case, *The Times* had described Roupell at the 1862 trial as being a remarkable performer on the criminal stage who had established his guilt by his courageous and straightforward eloquence. Readers were reminded of his theatrical address to the judge. A certain amount of sympathy towards him was apparent throughout this prolonged trial which was said to be an example of the skill, zeal and tenacity of the Bar and the patience of the judge and jury.

The final comment appeared at length on Tuesday 28th July. The trial was described as being full of paradoxes and with a paradoxical verdict. Roupell's persistence, the inability of the defence to break him down and the minor mysteries exposed were listed. Why had no-one questioned the large number of mortgages and conveyances executed in his father's lifetime without reference to him? Why did Mr Bovill not cross-examine Roupell on the detailed evidence he gave regarding the forgeries? Why was Sarah Roupell not asked directly about her father's signature on her letter? Why were more competent and obvious witnesses not called by either side? Why was the jury not given clear legal direction regarding the deed which they could neither accept as valid, nor yet agree was a fraud?

However, the final comment must come from *Punch*, August 8th 1863. 'In the great Roupell case the jury agreed that the Will was forged, but differed as to whether the Deed was genuine. Those of them who credit the genuineness of the latter document are of course prepared to deny that the Will is as good as the Deed.' Fortunately, the trial regarding the Roupell Park estate, scheduled for the following month at Croydon, did not take place.

THE FINAL YEARS

Roupell Park 1864 - 1909

William Roupell served the full life sentence of fourteen years, not being released until September 1876. His brother Richard spent about the same length of time trying to salvage what he could of his lost inheritance. After the public scandal of the trial, Mrs Roupell, Sarah and Richard returned to Aspen House. No evidence has been found of the humiliation and changes in lifestyle and financial circumstances they must have faced. However, newspaper reports and published letters about the affair were fairly favourable to William; these and William's later acceptance into the community suggest his family were regarded locally with some sympathy.

The Roupell story and William's prison progress continued to be followed in the press. In February 1864, a title dispute, Roupell v Doulton, was settled. This concerned Henry Doulton's Fore Street pipe factory, leased by Mrs Roupell and William to Doulton in 1854, with an option to purchase.

In October, *The Times* reported that 'The Porchester', a transport vessel, was to take two hundred convicts to serve their time in Gibraltar. One of these was to be William Roupell, but he avoided transportation because he was expected to be a witness at future trials. He was then employed as a labourer in the extension work at Chatham dockyard, described as dressed in a coarse grey convict suit and using a spade or pick-axe to dig stone, or pulling a cart, yoked to other prisoners.

Early in 1865, the press reported that there would be a re-trial at Chelmsford in order to reach a verdict, one way or the other, on the Warley estate, and therefore on the remainder of the Roupell estates. In June, coverage again told the Roupell background in preparation for this trial but, in July, it was stated that Richard Roupell and the occupiers of the property were to settle out of court. Richard Roupell's proposition, via his solicitor Linklater, was understood to be that he should receive half the value of the remaining estates, as had been accepted on Norbiton Park in 1862. Estimates put this at about £100,000. This was rejected and finally Richard was reported to have agreed to receive a total of about £50,000, in return for fresh deeds being executed in favour of the occupiers. His evidence being no longer required, William was expected to be transported to Bermuda, but he was in fact returned to Portland Prison, Dorset.

On Christmas Day 1865, under the heading 'William Roupell, ex-M.P, the Good Convict', the following report appeared: 'It is well known to the authorities of the convict establishment of Portland, and to all who dwell in the lower part of Dorset, that a great deal of what is technically called 'trafficking with the prisoners', which means communicating between convicts and their relatives, is carried on clandestinely through the instrumentality of the warders and other persons. It is very seldom, however, that these offenders against the prison regulations are detected. A conviction of this offence was obtained last Saturday at Dorchester, through the assistance of the ex-MP William Roupell, who has thereby earned a new claim to the title of 'an excellent prisoner', which the governor lately gave him.'

It appeared that a few days previously a warder named Turner, who had been employed at the establishment for upwards of seven years, sent a letter by one of the convicts to Roupell, intimating that his relatives had been imposed on by someone who had applied for money on his behalf, but that he (Turner) would serve him faithfully, and suggested that Roupell should write to his relatives for £10, which would enable him to get comforts which the prison authorities did not allow, and direct it to be sent to him by post-office order made payable to 'William Haig' at Weymouth. With this note a sheet of paper was enclosed.

Roupell, however, on receiving it, was annoyed to learn that his relatives had been imposed on by people pretending to apply for money for him, because he did not want anything from them. He showed the letter to the governor of the prison, by whose direction he then wrote a letter to his sister asking her to send £10, as Turner suggested, and he forwarded it to the warder by the convict who gave him the first note. Turner wrote on the fly sheet of Roupell's letter, recommending that Miss Roupell should send the £10 in two £5 notes. The governor also communicated with Miss Roupell, and the result was that she sent a post-office order for £5 to Turner, made payable as he wished. This he received on December 16th and he sent his wife to get it cashed. She told the clerk her husband's name was William Haig, and that he could not write, so she put her mark as signature to the order. Superintendent Underwood, of the county constabulary, went to Portland Prison, where Turner was on duty. The governor discharged him and he was taken into custody. The examination of Turner took place at Portland because Roupell and other prisoners were witnesses. Turner pleaded guilty and was sentenced to six months hard labour.

In March 1867 the mortgagees of Thundersley Lodge Farm in Essex applied to Richard Roupell for a total of £8,000, secured on the estate in 1861. In October the following year, the farm was sold for £11,300, which was £2,200 less than its estimated value in 1862.

On January 22nd 1869, *The Times* falsely reported that William Roupell had been freed on a ticket-of-leave (bail) because of the dangerous condition of his health, brought about by his confinement.

In1871, Richard Roupell entered into negotiations to settle the ownership of the three properties: Trunk Farm, near Farnborough in Hampshire, the land in Wandsworth and Roupell Park, Streatham. He retained Trunk Farm himself, the title of the Wandsworth land (mortgaged) was given to his sister Sarah, and Roupell Park was to be gradually sold off. Negotiations started on a large undeveloped section of Roupell Park, the site centring on the present Fenstanton School, to sell for £4,600 to Mark Shepherd, a local solicitor, who later built there a large house with extensive grounds.

The census entry of that year for Aspen House names Mrs Roupell, aged seventy-four, as the head of the household, her income being derived from rents; Richard, aged thirty, described as a barrister not in practice; and Sarah, aged thirty-seven. The staff comprised Elizabeth Dove, the seventy-four year old cook, a widow (probably of William's agent Joseph Dove), and a housemaid.

Roupell doing convict labour
Ilustrated Weekly News 4 Oct 1862

In February 1872, rights were given to the occupiers and tenants of the Roupell Street area, north Lambeth. On May 8th 1872, it was reported that Roupell had declined an offer of a ticket-of-leave. Evidently his health had improved and he preferred to remain in prison where, it was said, he had immense influence over the inmates, and was most patient and attentive to the sick. Two days later, *The Times* was requested to correct this report, stating that all applications for Roupell's release had been refused by the Secretary of State.

The following month it was reported that further property settlements were reached. Roupell Street, which William said had been left to him in the 1850 will which he had destroyed, was given up to the mortgagees. Roupell Park, which according to this will had been left to Richard, was settled in favour of Richard and William's mortgagees. The value of the two estates was said to be £240,000, sufficient to pay off the mortgagees and to satisfy Richard. William was reported to have willingly signed the relevant documents, expressing a desire to do all in his power to make reparation. In October Mrs Roupell made her will.

Through 1872 and 1873 sales continued on Roupell Park. Examining the deeds conveying a house in Roupell Park, something of the complexities involved at this time in proving ownership can be appreciated. Along with the plan of 39 Christchurch Road are: a plan of the Roupell Park estate in 1838, with accompanying statement dated 1855, a declaration identifying Mrs Roupell as Mrs Carter in Pitt Street, copies of statements and certificates of the births, baptisms and the two deaths of the Roupell children as well as the death of their father, his will and statements regarding the outcome of the 1862 trial.

On April 16th 1873, it was reported that a recommendation had been made to the Home Secretary that the convict Roupell appeared very ill and that this should be taken into account when the case for his early release be considered. One newspaper refuted reports that he was dying in Dartmouth convict infirmary, saying he was still at Portland where, although in delicate health, he was able to continue his usual occupation of bookbinding and was in reasonably good spirits. His conduct was described as excellent.

In 1873 the Great Warley land was sold followed in June 1874 by the sale of the Wandsworth land to WH Hewitt, the receiver for the Roupell Park estate, for £4,100; £1,500 being paid to Sarah Roupell. In August another part of Roupell Park was sold to a mortgagee.

In October Mr Bayne Rankin, hon. secretary to the Discharged Prisoners' Aid Society, wrote to *The Times* regarding Roupell's release. Reports had suggested this would be imminent because Roupell behaved well, touched his cap to the governor, impressed the chaplain, kept his cell clean and sang in a loud and devout voice in the prison chapel. Mr Rankin stated that early release depended on a man's industry in prison, not good conduct and the chaplain. The system had been settled by an Act of Parliament, applied by a judge, not by an arrangement between the Home Secretary, the gaol chaplain and the convict. In 1864, an Act had extended life sentences to twenty years; Roupell being sentenced before this date would be released after the statutory fourteen years, in 1876.

In May 1876, after further enquiry, the Wandsworth land was sold by the receiver WH Hewitt to the Eagle Insurance Company for £11,490, well above its sale price two years previously. On July 14th Richard Roupell made his will. On September

21st *The Times* reported the imminent release of William Roupell, whose conduct while in prison and his work, night and day, with the sick and the dying in the prison hospital were praised. On September 22nd, after fourteen years, he was released. Instead of taking the train at Portland, he was driven in a carriage to Weymouth station to avoid the crowd of observers expected at Portland. Shortly after his return to Streatham and to Aspen House, his local vicar, the Rev. Wodehouse Raven of Christ Church, walked arm-in-arm with Roupell around the parish to show his support. Later evidence suggests his brother Richard was not quite so welcoming.

By then, building work had recommenced to develop the Norwood half of the estate. That William's speculative investment in the estate could be said to have a sound basis, is reflected in contemporary accounts. In February 1878 the prime minister, Mr Gladstone, visited Roupell Park to look at the first successful experiments with a new steam tree-feller. William Roupell, with his long-term interest in horticulture, must surely have been present. A local newspaper reported the event and remarked that the estate was a striking example of the rapid increase in the value of land. In less than three years the price per acre had risen from £750 to £1,200 and houses which, six years ago, were difficult to let were now rapidly being added to by houses in various styles of architecture, from Tudor to Gothic, ranging in accommodation from nine to twenty rooms. Large trees were cut down to make way for the extensive building, and re-planting planned.

Eighteen months after William's release, on March 22nd 1878, he was present at the death of his mother Sarah, aged 81, at Aspen House. She was buried in the family vault in Norwood Cemetery a week later. Her will, proved on April 13th, left her estate, valued at £1,500, to her 'dear daughter called Sarah Roupell', the phrase used to denote an illegitimate child, as discussed at the trial with reference to William, allegedly thus named in his father's 1850 will. Apart from her solicitor, her executors were her daughter and the son of her husband's business colleague, Henry Muggeridge, surveyor, of St George's Place, Brixton. A codicil added in July 1876, a few days after her son Richard made his will, stated that she had made no bequest to Richard as she felt that he was amply provided for.

After her death, Aspen House was sold to William Yates Baker, iron master, art connoisseur and future maternal grandfather of the writer Dennis Wheatley. After Baker's death in 1916 his vast art collection was auctioned and Aspen House and grounds were sold. The house was demolished to make way for a tram shed (extant), built in 1923. The grounds were acquired by the London County Council to be used for an open-air school for 100 delicate children, Aspen House School. Later this became The Orchard Centre (Lambeth Education). The site now (2001) awaits development.

In his autobiography, *The Young Man Said*, Wheatley describes Aspen House as a square, three-storey block with two lower wings, cream-painted and containing about twenty rooms. He described the lawn with its two great old mulberry trees upon which he and, almost certainly, the young Roupells, used to climb. He listed the peach house, the tomato house, two other hot houses and two orchid houses. Further on was a large two-storey building with stables and coach house below (extant). Then came three potting sheds, a mushroom house, a chicken run, a walled kitchen garden, two orchards, a vinery, a summer house, an archery target and a swing. Much of this must have originated during Roupell's inhabitancy. Wheatley wrote that his grandfather used to allow William Roupell to come into the garden once a year when the fruit was ripe to pick as much as he wished. It is not difficult to imagine Roupell's feelings on entering the garden he loved and which he once thought of as his.

Aspen House being sold, William and his sister Sarah moved to Harvey Lodge, 2 Christchurch Road, adjacent to and east of Garden Lane. This semi-detached house was situated opposite Christ Church and in full view of the back of Aspen House and its grounds. In the 1881 census, Sarah, aged forty-seven, is described as the head of the house and a fund holder and William, aged forty-nine, and a retired barrister; a domestic servant lives in.

By then Richard Roupell had moved to his remaining property Trunk Farm, Hawley in Hampshire (house extant). His friend, neighbour and solicitor, James Harvie Linklater with his wife Isobel, moved to an adjacent house. As both households were listed in directories in 1878, it may be assumed that they were resident before this date. Perhaps Richard spent as little time as possible at Aspen House after his brother's release. In the 1881 census Richard Roupell, aged forty and unmarried, is described as a barrister at law (not in practice) and a farmer of 300 acres employing ten men, eleven boys and four women. Isobel Linklater, aged 57, is described as the head of her house.

Two years later, on March 2nd 1883, the unfortunate Richard Roupell, aged forty-two, of Trunk Farm, died of pneumonia at 2 Pierrepoint St (extant), Bath. The following week he was buried in the family vault at Norwood. Interestingly, it was a year before his will was proved, suggesting ownership of the Roupell properties was still not settled. His will had not been altered since it was drawn up in 1876 and makes fascinating reading. To a friend George Frederick Rumford of Lower Norwood he left £300, to two others he left £50 each with which to purchase a ring in his memory. To his employee W Woodley he left £100, his horses, carriages, saddling and tools at Aspen House. To the Infant Orphan Asylum, Wanstead (now Snaresbrook Crown Court) and the Asylum for Idiots, Redhill, he left £200 each. To his mother and sister he left annuities of £200. To his friend Mrs Isobel Frances Linklater he left £5,000 and to her son, Frederick Harvie Linklater, he left £200.

His mother and heirs (her daughter Sarah) were left the stabling and orchard, adjoining the garden of Aspen House. During her lifetime she was left Boylands Oak Farm at Stapleford Abbots, all other Essex properties, and Daphne Cottage, adjacent to Aspen House. After his mother's death, Daphne Cottage was willed to his sister

Sarah, and Boylands Oak Farm to Isobel Linklater. Mrs Linklater was also left the family home, Boylands Oak in Streatham, leased from the Roupells. Her husband, James Harvie Linklater, was left Trunk Farm and any remaining estate. The will was proved on March 28th 1884, the estate being valued at £13,225, proved to Linklater. By this time, little more than Daphne Cottage, the stabling and orchard, Boylands Oak at Streatham and Trunk Farm in Hampshire could have been in his possession. Subsequently the Linkláters moved to Bournemouth.

Boylands Oak, Brixton Hill c. 1905.

But the most interesting bequest was that made by Richard to his brother William: 'To William Roupell, now a convict in Portland Prison, in the event of his being released from his imprisonment, an annuity of £52, to be paid by equal weekly payments.' This, of course, matched the allowance William had received from his father thirty years earlier and which, he had alleged at his trial, was insufficient for his needs and had therefore led to his first forgery. This bequest must disprove allegations that the brothers were involved in a scheme to deprive owners of their legitimately purchased properties. This surely is evidence to show that William Roupell's story of his forgeries was true, at least in the main, and that the bitterness felt by his brother in losing his inheritance and the family's reputation never left him.

William and Sarah continued to live in quiet respectability, presumably renting Harvey Lodge with the proceeds of the sale of Daphne Cottage, her income supplementing his £1 a week. William became very much involved in local activities. He was particularly associated with Christ Church, the church for which his father had sold the plot of land and led the procession, as one of the major sponsors, at the ceremony to lay the foundation stone. Ironically, he became secretary of the Christ Church Slate Club, being responsible for significant sums of money. He became a keen gardener - he told someone that he had begun gardening at three years of age - and now he took up work in a friend's nursery garden, near his home at the top of Garden Lane. Since his release, he was variously described in the census and directories as a retired barrister, an estate agent and surveyor and, by 1891, a consulting horticulturist.

He became secretary and, later, president of the Brixton, Streatham and Clapham Horticultural Society of which he was a founder member when MP, particularly enjoying helping to organise their exhibitions. In the archives of the Tate Gallery in London are two letters of condolence written in December 1899 by William Roupell, as secretary of both the Slate Club and the Horticultural Society, to Lady Tate on the death of her husband, Sir Henry Tate of Park Hill, Streatham, the sugar magnate, art collector and benefactor of the Tate Gallery and the Tate libraries in Lambeth.

By this time, although still a fashionable area in which to live, the slow demise of Roupell Park as a middle-class residential area had begun. The largest new house, Fenstanton, was auctioned to a local butcher in 1890 but by 1899 was leased to a doctor who used it as a nursing home. The second phase of building to Norwood Road was complete, the houses being less grand, many occupied by local tradesmen. The proximity to London via the nearby Tulse Hill and Streatham Hill railway stations led to an increasing density of population and the wealthier middle classes started moving into more rural parts. By the 1900s, many of the larger houses were divided into flats or were private schools or nursing homes.

On July 12th 1894, Roupell was present at the death of his sister Sarah, aged sixty, from 'diabetes and general exhaustion'. She also was buried in the family vault. Her will left her total estate, £126 14s 11d, to William. In the event of his pre-decease, she mentions her father's cousins who were related via her grandmother Catherine Roupell (née Brand). They were the Hollington family who owned a market garden in Dagenham, Essex. These appear to have been the only Roupell relatives known to Sarah and Richard. They lived in the south Essex area where Richard Palmer Roupell bought various farms and from where his mother Catherine had originated and inherited money. Sarah's will, drawn up in 1892, was witnessed by Arthur Wood, gardener, of Upper Orchard Street, Lyham Road, Brixton Hill. Wood is recorded living at that address in 1891, aged twenty-eight, with his wife Ellen and a baby daughter.

William Roupell's address continued to be Harvey Lodge; however, this was not the house he shared with Sarah, later to be known as Harvey House, but a small cottage opposite in Garden Lane, which Roupell presumably renamed. He was cared for by the aforementioned Arthur and Ellen Wood.

It is not clear who owned Harvey Lodge; newspaper reports on Roupell's death said it belonged to 'a friend'. However, it appears to be the former Roupell estate office, inhabited originally by the Roupell's farm bailiff Joseph Dove, who is recorded there in 1851 and 1861. It was in the Roupells' possession at least until the break-up of the estate in 1878 after Mrs Roupell's death. It was described later as a gardener's cottage with four rooms. Mrs Wood, later a widow, rented Harvey Lodge until 1933. She was described as a very kind and good woman who felt much sympathy for Roupell and cared for him for some fourteen years until his death.

Mrs Wood's granddaughter and a niece remember Harvey Lodge and conversations about William Roupell. They describe the cottage as being detached, slate-roofed, facing Garden Lane, and with a high brick wall, all built in yellow stock brick. A gate led into the courtyard to the front of the house which was covered with white jasmine. The nursery garden nearby contained raspberries, vines and fruit trees. This apparently was owned by a Mr Herring of Streatham Hill, who allowed Roupell to work there until his death. Arthur Wood either rented the garden or was employed there.

A local resident described Roupell as being a very short man with grey hair curling on his shoulders and always wearing a sealskin cape. A later obituary described him as a venerable figure, affable and genial, always willing to help those around him and whose erudition made him an agreeable conversationalist. His considerable church work was noted. He was described as a horticulturist of no mean repute, who was famous for his choice grapes until French competition compelled him to devote his attention principally to apples, which he grew to perfection. He was an expert in fruit culture, frequently giving lectures on the subject to his horticultural society. Despite his success at selling his produce locally, he never made a profit of more than 10s (50p) a week. He never seems to have been a successful businessman.

Mrs Wood's daughter spoke of him as being a dear old man, of whom her family was enormously fond. On her seventeenth birthday, Roupell gave her a tiny ring with a garnet surrounded by pearls, which she wore on her little finger, and which is still in the family. It is believed the ring once belonged to William's sister, Sarah. She was also very excited to be taken by Roupell for a birthday celebration lunch at Romano's restaurant. Her daughter, Mrs Wood's granddaughter, says everyone said he was a real charmer. She understood her grandmother burned all Roupell's old diaries, at his request, when he died. She believes his last years were very happy and tranquil. Apart from the ring, several other mementoes remain in her family, including a cameo brooch, books, a self-portrait of Richard Palmer Roupell, an inscribed glass goblet and a prayer book inscribed, 'To Arthur Wood from William Roupell. Presented to George Arthur Wood, 29th July 1904'. A miniature of Sarah Roupell was lost some time ago.

These were William Roupell's only possessions to give away before he died intestate on March 25th 1909, aged 77, of pneumonia and heart failure, at a private nursing home at 50 Salford Road, Streatham Hill (extant), to where he had been taken three weeks earlier. His death certificate described him as a consulting horticulturist of Harvey Lodge.

The Times reported his death and funeral, and gave a long account of the trials. The report of his funeral service on March 29th at Christ Church described the removal of the oak coffin, covered in beautiful wreaths, from Harvey Lodge. The service was conducted by the vicar, the Rev. CS Nichol, and about three hundred people were present; school children from the Sunday School were in the gallery. It was said few people knew of his past, but those who did recognised he had atoned for his crime and had won great respect in the district. A wreath was sent by 'three old non-commissioned officers', early members of Roupell's Volunteer regiment. Other wreaths came from local tradesmen, the children and teachers of the Sunday School, members of the Slate Club and the Horticultural Society.

On the same day a letter from the Rev. Nichol was published in *The Times* in support of Roupell. He said that in the eighteen years he had been vicar at Christ Church he knew William Roupell as an earnest and regular communicant, who was much respected in the neighbourhood. He described how his predecessor had welcomed Roupell back into the community on his release from prison. He recounted his struggle to survive financially and his work with the church, including helping the children to observe Empire Day, and his membership of the Guild of Intercession.

The Streatham News described his funeral in more detail. It reported a congregation of between four and five hundred at the event, but with no relatives, as he had outlived them all. The cortege arrived with ten mourning coaches at about noon, passing through lines of schoolchildren and their teachers. The more important guests were listed, including Ronald Doulton, of the pottery family. A large number of ladies were present. The service opened with the 19th psalm. Afterwards the procession made its way to Norwood Cemetery for interment of the body in the family vault. Whether through oversight or lack of money, William Roupell's name was not inscribed on the tomb plate along with the rest of his family and his mother's sister, Leah.

Obituaries were published, both nationally and locally, recounting his public life and shame, his exciting campaign at the last hustings election in Lambeth, and his subsequent thirty-three years of the 'simple life'. One described him in his everlasting black frock coat and shovel hat, with a benevolent appearance, a quiet gentlemanly bearing, kindly eyes, a broad intelligence and succinct wisdom. The writer described a visit to his home and being welcomed by Roupell, although he was in the middle of a frugal mid-day meal, which he had cooked for himself. The only furniture was a table and chairs and he was surrounded by heaps of potatoes, apples and onions.

Roupell took his guest to the garden and talked of methods of grafting and propagation. He evidently did not believe in pruning his fruit trees. He had once given a lecture on fruit growing at the Doulton's Institute. The writer commented that the Doultons had remained friends of Roupell since before his election campaign.

In *The Brixton Free Press* a long appreciation of Roupell described his funeral in rather fulsome detail as being on a beautiful spring day. It attacked the 'vampires of the Press' who had 'rummaged in the dust heap of the past and dragged forth into the garish light of day the sin of long ago'. It commented that the local children would 'look in vain for his kindly presence and cheery word'.

A local man, Claude Greening, wrote the following:

VALE!
WILLIAM ROUPELL, LAID TO REST
MARCH 29th.

Your life was well prolonged beyond the span
Allotted, as the Psalmist says, to man.
Your Maker knew how contrite was your heart,
But human minds play such a narrow part
That many in their pride refused to you
The meed of honour that was justly due.
A worker for the Church you long had been
Ere God did call you to a fairer scene;
And those who knew you, whatsoe'er their age
Or what the part they played upon life's stage,
Respected you and held you in regard.
Farewell, true Christian! Man is cold and hard,
But Christ is boundless mercy, boundless love -
And you have found Him in the great above.

So what remains of the Roupells? At the time of writing, only five of the original houses of Roupell Park remain: two in Palace Road and three on Streatham Hill. Most of the post-1880 housing remains. The boundary of the estate is quite obvious along present property divides. Parts of the original walls remain. The Orchard Centre (awaiting development), Christ Church, and the three roads - Christchurch, Palace and Roupell - are all extant. The Roupell Park Methodist Church, on Norwood Road, was bombed, but a replacement was sited behind. The present Roupell Park Estate has the name but not the location, being to the north of the boundary of the old estate.

In Westminster and the City, the narrow and winding Strutton Ground and Shoe Lane recall earlier generations. The Roupell Street area of Lambeth is externally almost intact. The workers' houses are now in a conservation area and considered very desirable dwellings. Bear Lane and a sign Gravel Lane (Great Suffolk Street) remain, and a walk around the area shows some evidence of its industrial past, including continued scrap-metal dealing. The Wandsworth estate has mainly been replaced by flats, but the boundary along Wandsworth, Wilcox, Thorncroft and Hartington Roads remains.

In Essex, Chelmsford Assizes can still be seen. Boylands Oak Farm, Stapleford Abbots, has recently been demolished or renovated; some of the farmland remains. Thundersley Lodge remains, as does some of the farmland. The old estate was rectangular, bounded on two sides by the present A13 and A129. In Great Warley, the old farmhouse, now Berry Lodge, and the newer Victorian Bury Farm House (now listed) remain, the surrounding area mainly still farmland. In Surrey, the Norbiton Park estate boundary can be seen along Kingston Road, South Lane and Thetford Road. In Hampshire, old Trunk Farm, near Farnborough, is an industrial estate, but Richard Roupell's land and home, Trunk House, remain, as do the nearby Linklater's cottages.

Intriguingly, there is a Roupell House (a modern residential home), not far from the site of Norbiton Park Farm, and another, a block of flats in Lisford Road, on an estate in Peckham, not far from the site of the Pitt Street house where William Roupell spent his early years. Evidence has not been found of any Roupell connection with these sites.

The family vault of Richard Palmer Roupell, as inscribed round the edge of the slab, remains, but without the brass name plate. It lies, with a yew tree at each corner, on top of the hill in West Norwood Cemetery, in sight of the flats of St Martin's Estate on the opposing hill which was once Roupell Park. Of course, the Central Criminal Court in Old Bailey, the arena of William Roupell's public downfall, remains just a short walk from Shoe Lane, where William's father, grandparents, great-grandparents and great-great grandparents lived and built up the family fortune which he lost.

William Roupell 1831-1909

ROUPELL CHRONOLOGY

1688 *November 5th* - William Prince of Orange landed at Brixham to claim English throne.

1689 CONRAD (Roepel), Captain, William III's Guard, married DINAH.

August 26th - granted pension.

1690 *June 28th* - son WILLIAM baptised Savoy Chapel.

1691 *February 16th* - CONRAD Groom of Ewry in Royal Household.

1693 *November 16th* - daughter Dinah baptised Savoy Chapel.

1695 *August 1st* - son JOHN baptised Savoy Chapel.

1699 *January 13th* - son Charles baptised Savoy Chapel.

1700 *March 10th* - twins Anna and Philip baptised.

October 5th - son Peter baptised.

1705 *December 31st* - CONRAD died Germany. Address Strutton Ground, Westminster.

1706 *January 30th* - Probate to wife DINAH.

1713 Eldest son WILLIAM married wealthy widow Sarah Whitfield.

1716 *October 4th* - son Philip, of St Margaret's Westminster, apprenticed to coachmaker.

1718 *May 13th* - DINAH arranged a money loan and signed promissory notes by this date.

1721 *March 18th* - Dinah declared bankrupt, 7 year certificate.

October 19th - son Peter ensign 38th Foot (S.Staffs), then in West Indies. Not in 1727 Army List.

1723 *November 13th* - WILLIAM (33), widower, married Anne Towley, Chapel Royal, Whitehall.

1726 *March 5th* - DINAH arrested for debt and imprisoned in Holland.

October 5th - DINAH released on bail, fled to England.

1727 *May 31st* - DINAH arrested for contempt of court; later released. Listed receiving pension from Royal Household.

173? JOHN married PATIENCE.

1733 JOHN, son JOHN and PATIENCE, born. Late in year DINAH visited niece in Holland.

1736 *March* - DINAH, late of Kensington, now Brentford, instigated Chancery proceedings for wrongful arrest.

   May 26th - judgement in her favour.

1737 *June 21st* - further action against DINAH for costs failed.

   October 25th - Mary, daughter JOHN & PATIENCE of Shoe Lane, baptised St Andrew's, Holborn

1740 *March 23rd* - William, son JOHN & P, baptised St Andrew's (infant death?).

   July - DINAH of Shoe Lane died, *November 22nd* buried St Andrew's.
   JOHN listed Bangor Court.

1741 *January 1st* - DINAH's probate to son JOHN.

1742 William, son JOHN & P, born.

1743 *January 1st* - William baptised St Andrew's.

1752 JOHN of Dolphin Court listed jeweller of Ludgate Hill.

1759 *October 14th* - JOHN (son J&P) married MARY Canter at St Pancras Old Church.

   December 23rd - JOHN, husband of PATIENCE, buried St Martin's, Ludgate.

1761 *April 16th* - JOHN, son JOHN & MARY of Field Lane, baptised St Andrew's.

   Widow RUPELL (sic) taxed Dolphin Court.

1762 *May 19th* - PATIENCE buried St Martin's Ludgate.

1763 *February 17th* - William buried St Martin's.

   November 3rd - Thomas Edward son JOHN & MARY born,

   November 18th - baptised St Martin's.

1764 JOHN taxed Dolphin Court.

1765 *March 17th* - James Cecil, son J & M born,

   April 11th - baptised, *April 28th* - buried St Martin's.

1766 *November 16th* - Mary Rebeckah, daughter J & M, born.

   December 16th - bapt. St Martin's.

1767 JOHN taxed Stonecutter St.

1777 *December 24th* - JOHN, husband MARY, buried St Bride's.

1779 Widow ROUPELL taxed Stonecutter St.

1781 *May 30th* - JOHN married CATHERINE BRAND at St Bride's.

1782 *February 21st* - RICHARD PALMER son J & C born.

      March 21st - baptised St Bride's.

1783 *October 26th* - MARY, widow of JOHN, married Timothy Plaw at St Andrew-by-Wardrobe.

1785 *March 27th* - Mary Rebeckah, daughter J & M, married James Brand, CATHERINE's brother.

1791 CATHERINE received bequest from aunt Ann Osborne's estate

1796 *November 18th* - Roupell St deed of 1880 refers to 99-year lease from this date (to JOHN?).

1800 *(circa)* JOHN established Bear Lane factory.

1810 *August 21st* - JOHN, of Cuper's Bridge, bought land from Lord Thurlow's Brixton Hill estate.

1811 JOHN bought two cottages formerly Brixton Hill Farm and part Knight's Hill estate.

1813 JOHN ROUPELL rated 25 acres, late Lord Thurlow's estate, Water Lane, Brixton Hill.

1815 *(circa)* JOHN living at 16 Cross St.

1817 RICHARD PALMER ROUPELL listed engine-maker and millsmith of Bear Lane.

1818 JR rated barn and land Streatham. RPR bought future Garden Lane area in trust for JR.

1819 JR of Cross St bought more land from Lord Thurlow's estate.

1820 *March* - RPR Wandsworth Rd 14 yr lease. JR rated dwelling Cross St, 5 houses Broadwall.

1821 Deeds Glasshouse Yard, Gravel Lane, to JR.

1822 Wandsworth land assigned to RPR

1823 JR listed lead-ash smelter 16 Cross St and smith 33 Bear Lane. Rated Princes Square: 6 tenanted houses, Broadwall: house and yard. RPR listed Cornwall Rd: house, factory and land.

1824 JR leased The Grove (junction Ewer, Lavington Streets). Roupell Street development started.

June - Wandsworth land leased to builders, developed over 6 yrs.

1826 *January 5th* - JOHN born, son RPR & SARAH CRANE, address Clarendon St, Somers Town.

February - JOHN baptised St Pancras, (RPR age 43, SC age 29).

JR anchorsmith, Bear Lane.

1828 JR listed lead smelter, Gravel Lane; wrought iron manufacturer, Bear Lane with house.

October 17th - Leah Crane (age 23) baptised All Souls, Langham Place.

1829 *February* - JR sold land for Union Chapel, later Streatham Hill Congregational Church, now Brixton Hill United Reform Church.

June - JR & RPR sold land for St Ann's Society, Streatham. JR rated Lambeth, Roupell buildings: 27 tenanted houses, 35 houses, yard and house, stable and yard. RPR rated Cornwall Rd house, factory and land.

1831 *April 7th* - WILLIAM born, son RPR and SC, (Pitt St, Peckham?).

1832 JR building licence to EH Day plot N of Union Chapel, Brixton Hill.

1833 *October 21st* - SARAH born, daughter RPR & SC.

November 30th - baptised St Giles, Camberwell.

1834 JR listed iron foundry Bear Lane and lead works Dyers Buildings, Gravel Lane.

1835 JR listed lead works 33 Bear Lane and iron foundry 32 Gravel Lane.

November - JR leased to S Smith land present Perran Rd, Tulse Hill.

December 23rd - JOHN ROUPELL 'of Roupell St' died.

1836 *January 2nd* - JOHN buried St John's Waterloo.

February 5th - admon to RPR £25,000.

May 7th - CATHERINE made will.

June and Nov - Roupell Park and Stapleford Abbots assigned to RPR. Norbiton Park held in trust.

73 houses listed Roupell Street area.

1837 *February 10th* - EMMA born, daughter RPR & SC.

1838 *February 27th* - CATHERINE died, buried St John's.

May 7th - will proved to RPR: £12,000, value of annuities and bequests over £9,000.

December 6th - RPR married SARAH St Giles Church, Camberwell.

1839 Roupell buildings, 82 houses etc. *January* - Norbiton Park transferred to RPR.

February 10th - At St George's Camberwell, John and Sarah received, William and Emma baptised.

October - RPR sold land for Christ Church, Streatham Hill.

November - Thundersley, Essex, conveyance. RPR made will.

SARAH and children remove to Aspen House, Brixton Hill.

1840   *July 27th* - RICHARD born, legitimate son RPR and SR. RPR made will benefiting him.

October - RPR bought Trunk Farm, Hants.

1841   Deeds of a pottery in Fore St to RPR.

1842   *June* - Roupell St area appears complete.

July - Laindon and Great Warley, Essex; land lease to RPR.

New Bury Farm House built.

1843   Leah Crane (38) died Aspen House.

1844   *March* - Christchurch Road laid out.

October - Boylands Oak building lease, adjacent to Aspen House.

RPR made new will.

1845   *November 2nd* - RICHARD (age 5) baptised Christ Church.

1847   WILLIAM (16/17) enters business, (RPR 65).

1849   WILLIAM articled as clerk to Haslam & Rees until 1854.

1850   RPR willed Norbiton Park, Roupell Park and Great Warley to RICHARD (10).

February 2nd - WR's first fraud: to mortgage Norbiton Park.

August - RPR Trunk Farm, Hants, purchase completed.

1852   Boylands Oak, Brixton Hill, leased to Linklater.

1853   *August* - WR mortgaged Norbiton Park.

September - in debt to uncle Watts, forged deed Roupell Park to self via mother.

November and December - loans to WR on Roupell Park.

1854   RPR sold land for St Andrew's Church, Coin St.

January - WR mortgaged Roupell Park.

August 24th - Fore St lease to Doulton for drainpipe pottery.

1855   WR kept father's cheque to buy land in Streatham Hill from John Treadwell. Further mortgage on plot E of Garden Lane (the first Harvey Lodge site).

April and July - WR mortgaged Great Warley & Norbiton Park. Lant St property listed.

WR (24) elected member Lambeth Vestry.

1856 *January and February* - Great Warley & Roupell Park further mortgaged.

7 acres and 2 cottages leased to Roupells by Treadwell of Leigham Court.

June and July - further advances on Roupell Park and Norbiton Park. Plan to continue Christchurch Rd to Norwood Rd and extend Trinity Rd (Hillside).

September 12th - RPR died, *September 18th* - buried Norwood Cemetery.

September 24th - will (forged) proved WR to mother SR, estate £120,000.

1857 *March 11th* - WR stood for parliament.

March 30th - elected Liberal MP for Lambeth.

May/June - critical pamphlet from 'A Lambeth Elector'.

July 10th - Committee of inquiry.

July 15th (?) -WR held Lambeth Festival, Surrey Gardens.

July 23rd - Warley mortgage.

July 31st - Fore St pottery sold to Doultons.

August - WR's plans for his new house and grounds at Roupell Park, site present Lanercost Rd.

October - Lant St mortgage, Trunk Farm deed of gift.

December 7th - Roupell St area sold.

December 9th - EMMA died Hastings, *14th* - death registered, *16th* - buried Norwood Cemetery.

1858 *June 25th* - WR spoke in House of Commons.

July - WR mortgaged Trunk Farm.

1859 *April* - WR re-elected M.P.

May and September - Warley and Trunk Farm mortgaged.

1860 WR established 'The Brixton Hill, Streatham, Clapham and Balham Amateurs' and Gardeners' Horticultural and Floricultural Society'.

February and March - WR chaired meetings to establish Lambeth Volunteer Corps.

June 28th - Volunteers inaugurated.

Further mortgage on Warley. Building ceased on Roupell Park estate.

1861   *February 28th* - death JOHN (35) hotel Adderley St, Port Elizabeth, South Africa.

Thundersley money received. Wandsworth Rd property mortgaged.

March drill - WR absent, 'indisposed for some time'.

April onwards - much Volunteer activity, including *May 20th* - WR's report and dinner.

July 27th - RICHARD of age (21).

October - WR sold Norbiton Park to Waite.

1862   *February 4th* - resignation of officers.

March - WR tried to raise more money.

March 28th Friday -WR told mother he had money troubles.

March 29th - WR burned deeds in Kennington rooms.

March 30th - WR absconded to Spain.

April 7th - WR resigned from Volunteers.

May 5th - Bye-election to Doulton.

August 17th - WR at Richmond Church.

August 18th & 19th - WR arrested at Kingston; litigation starts. Roupell (Richard) & Others v. Waite, Guildford. Then WR to Horsemonger Goal, Southwark, to await trial at the Central Criminal Court.

September 13th - Ellice (Ellis) v Roupell, re Roupell Park deed of gift. Deferred for other verdicts.

September 22nd - Trial at Central Criminal Court. WR in Newgate gaol. WR moved to Pentonville after trial.

1863   *February* - Waite paid half value of Norbiton estate to RR, renamed Waitelands.

July 16th-24th - Roupell & Others v Haws & Others.

December 17th - Waite died.

1864   Roupell v Doulton re Fore St .

October - WR, working at Chatham Docks, avoids deportation pending future action.

1865   *June* - possible Essex litigation avoided; settled out of court.

December - WR 'good convict' report.

1867   Thundersley Lodge payment demand to Richard Roupell.

1868   Thundersley Lodge sold.

1869   *January 22nd* - false report of WR's release.

1871   RR living at Trunk Farm?

        July - Wandsworth land conveyance RR to sister SR.

1872   *May* - Roupell St settlement. False report WR to be released on bail.

        August - RR sold Fenstanton plot, Christchurch Rd, to M Shepherd. Agreement to sell Aspen House after mother's death. Warley estate sold.

1873   Roupell Park building recommenced.

1874   *June* - £1,500 to Sarah Roupell (jnr) from Wandsworth property sale.

        August - Roupell Park sold. WR release denied.

1876   Wandsworth land sold.

        July 14th - RR made will.

        September 22nd - WR released.

1878   *March 22nd* - SARAH (mother) died (81) at Aspen House, WR present.

        March 29th - SR buried Norwood Cemetery.

        Aspen House sold to WY Baker. SR and WR remove to Harvey Lodge, 2 Christchurch Rd. RR and Linklater listed at Hawley, Hants.

1879   RR sold rest Roupell Park E of Fenstanton (to Hardel Rise) to M Shepherd, owner of Fenstanton.

1883   *March 2nd* - RR (42) died Bath,

        March 9th - RR buried Norwood Cemetery.

1884   *March 28th* RR's will proved to Linklaters, including Boylands Oak Farm, Stapleford Abbots.

1890   *May 28th* - Fenstanton auctioned to Parsons, a local butcher.

1894   *July 12th* - SARAH (60) died 2 Christchurch Rd,

        July 18th - SARAH buried Norwood Cemetery.

        August 29th - will to WR.

1909   *March 25th* - WILLIAM died (77) intestate, 50 Salford Rd.

        March 29th - WILLIAM buried Norwood Cemetery.

PROPERTY

LONDON

SHOE LANE. Rents collected by John and RP Roupell, not located. 1856 premises' estimated value £2,000. 18thC & 19thC Roupells listed at Bangor Court, (off Shoe Lane), Shoe Lane and Stonecutter Street.

LAMBETH - NORTH

BROADWALL (then extended to Roupell St). 1823 house and yard listed (start of Roupell Street development?) (near borough boundary, see Southwark).

CORNWALL ROAD. 1823 RP Roupell listed house, factory and land. 1854 plot between Prince's (Coin) St and Cornwall Rd sold for building of St Andrew's Church (now demolished).

CUPER'S BRIDGE. 1810 John Roupell listed here (Cornwall Rd site?).

FORE STREET. 1841 pottery and buildings leased to RP Roupell. 1854 leased then 1857 sold to Henry Doulton for drainpipe factory. 1864 title dispute.

PRINCES SQUARE (now Cleaver Square?). 1823 six houses tenanted.

ROUPELL STREET estate, including Theed Street (John St), Whittlesey Street (east - Catherine St, west - Richard St). c1824 area developed on former Curtis's Hatch site. 1856 estimated value £50,000. 1857 Roupell Street area was sold for £27,586 12s. 1872 sold after title dispute. Externally mainly extant.

LAMBETH - SOUTH (then SURREY)

ROUPELL PARK estate, including Christchurch and Palace Roads. Rectangular site bounded by Streatham Hill, south to Pullman Court; Brixton Hill, north to Holmewood Gardens area; east to the north of Christchurch Road, including Gaywood Close, Fenstanton School and

Perran Road to Norwood Road; Leigham Vale to Kingsmead Avenue, and between Palace and Wavertree Roads. 1810-20 Roupells bought parcels of land from Lord Thurlow's estate, known as Knights/Brixton/Streatham Hills. 1829 Roupells sold land for Union Chapel, later Streatham Hill Congregational Church (modern replacement) and St Anne's Society Royal Asylum, site Pullman Court today. 1837 land adjacent to Union Chapel site leased for building to EH Day. 1839 Aspen House was built and other building started. 1839/40 land was sold for the building of Christ Church. 1844 Christchurch Road was laid out to Tulse Hill. 1853, 1854, 1855, 1856 mortgaged by William Roupell. 1856 estimated value £50,000, but later revised to £135,000; that of Aspen House being £400. 1860 building ceased, then recommenced in 1873 as various land ownership disputes were settled. Today extant: Christ Church, two buildings (c1840) on Streatham Hill, two in Palace Road and most post 1875 dwellings (mainly in Norwood half). The Aspen House site, the tram-shed and the Orchard Centre, with its Grade II* listed open-air classrooms, await development (2001).

SOUTHWARK

BOROUGH Hop warehouses (not identified). 1856 estimated value £2,500.

BROADWALL. 1820 five houses tenanted. 1856 estimated value £500.

BEAR LANE. c1800 at no 33 John Roupell established house and factory. Site now mainly covered by railway?

CROSS STREET, now Meymott St. c1815-1856 house no 16, office and yard home of John and Richard Palmer Roupell .

GRAVEL LANE area, now Great Suffolk St (northern part to junction Bear Lane). 1820 Glasshouse Yard deeds from then. 1824 lease the Grove/Winchester Park (junction Ewer and Lavington Sts?). 1834 Dyers Buildings listed (junction Bear and Gravel Lanes?). 1856 estimated value of lead works in Gravel lane £1,500.

LANT STREET. listed 1855. 1856 estimated value £3,500. 1857 mortgaged by William Roupell.

WANDSWORTH (then SURREY)

WANDSWORTH ROAD. Five acres off Wandsworth Road bounded by present Hartington, Wilcox and Thorncroft Rds (roads renamed). 1820 bought, 1824-30 leased to builders. 1856 estimated value £8,000. 1861 William Roupell granted leases to Henry Muggeridge, builder, and mortgaged land. 1874 sold after title disputes for £4,100 to WH Hewitt, receiver, who sold to WH Muggeridge in 1877 (for £11,490?).

ESSEX

GREAT WARLEY. 1842 Bury Farm (250 acres) and Bolens Farm (89 acres) bought. Bury Farm House subsequently built near to the old farmhouse, Bury House (Berry Lodge). Both extant. 1856 estimated value £12,000. 1855, 1856, 1857, 1859 and 1860 estate mortgaged by William Roupell. 1863 trial tenant farmer Daniel Haws. 1872 farm sold .

HAVERING-ATTE-BOWYER/STAPLEFORD ABBOTS. 1836 RP Roupell bought twenty acres, mainly wasteland. 1856 estimated value £7,500. 1862 James Surridge tenant farmer of Boylands Oak Farm listed. Richard Roupell willed this to his mother during her lifetime, then to Isobel Linklater. Farmhouse recently renovated or demolished.

THUNDERSLEY/LAINDON. 1839 RP Roupell bought Thundersley Lodge and two farms (299 acres). 1856 estimated value £10,000. Included was Marsh Farm (122 acres) in Laindon. 1859 WS Dean, tenant farmer of Thundersley Lodge, undertook considerable repairs and alterations. 1861 mortgaged by William Roupell. 1868 sold to Joseph Foster of Witham for £11,300. Site and old village in rectangle bounded on two sides by A13 and A129. Thundersley Lodge extant.

HAMPSHIRE

TRUNK FARM, Yately, Farnborough. 1840 RP Roupell bought for £3,266 9s 3d. 1856 estimated value £4,500. Trunk Farm (198 acres), Whitehouse Farm (75 acres), Gravett Hill (39 acres). 1858 and 1859 mortgaged by William Roupell. 1871 Richard Roupell proved title. By 1879, his address is given as Trunk Farm, farming 300 acres, with Isobel Linklater listed as a neighbour. Richard willed farm to his solicitor JH Linklater. By 1940 old Trunk farm was an army barracks, then an industrial estate. Trunk House, Trunk Road (Richard's home) and Linklater's Cottages, Minely Rd, extant.

SURREY

NORBITON PARK (FARM) estate. site bounded by Kingston Rd, South Lane and Thetford Rd. 1836/38 bought by RP Roupell. 1850, 1853, 1855 and 1856 mortgaged by W Roupell. 1856 estimated value £15,000. 1861 sold to John George Waite, 1862 title trial, settled out of court. 1863 Waite paid £7,500 (half the value) to Richard Roupell. Re-named Waitelands. 1863 Waite planned a railway through the land but died. 1865 auctioned for £29,000.

SOUTHWELL (Southville, Lambeth?) (1856 estimated value £4,500) not identified.

THE PEOPLE

A list, outside the immediate family, of those who were part of William Roupell's story.

BAKER William Yates: iron master and maternal grandfather of author Dennis Wheatley, bought Aspen House after Sarah Roupell's (mother) death.

BARNES Messrs: contracted to lay out roads on Roupell Park in 1856.

BRAND Catherine: daughter of Mary and Thomas, below. Married John Roupell in 1781.

BRAND James: hearth rug manufacturer, brother of Catherine Roupell, above. In 1785 married Mary Rebecca, sister to John Roupell, his brother-in-law.

BRAND Mary: née Woodford, wife of Thomas, below. Maternal family Palmer, yeoman farmers of Writtle, near Chelmsford, Essex. RP Roupell's maternal grandmother.

BRAND Thomas: wine merchant, of Apps Court, Walton-on-Thames. Father of Catherine Roupell, née Brand, and James. RP Roupell's maternal grandfather.

BRISTOWE Robert: with Pattison Nickalls he brought a petition questioning W Roupell's 1857 election campaign. 1860 listed as renting Daphne Cottage, adjacent to Aspen House, from the Roupells.

BOVILL Mr: MP QC, senior counsel for Waite 1862 and Haws 1863 trials with Hawkins QC and Garth. In 1856 Bovill had acted for W Roupell in Whittington v Roupell.

BYLES Mr Justice: sentenced W Roupell at the Central Criminal Court.

CALDWELL: female servant at Aspen House. Witness at 1863 trial.

CHABOT, MATHESON and NETHERCLIFT: expert lithographers, witnesses at 1863 trial.

CLARKE William: Roupell's rent collector, one of RP Roupell's executors and trustees. Witness at 1863 trial.

COMFORT G: butcher of Farringdon Market, an executor of John Roupell's will.

CRANE Leah: Sarah Roupell's sister. Born c1805. Baptised 1828 All Saint's Church, Langham Place. Died 1843 at Aspen House.

CRANE Sarah: née Harvey, of Stoke Ash, Suffolk, wife of Thomas (below) and mother of Sarah Roupell, Maria Watts and Leah.

CRANE Thomas: a carpenter, husband of Sarah (above), father of Sarah, Maria and Leah.

DAY Edward: schoolmaster, of Clapham and Cleveland House, Brixton Hill. 1832 leased land from Roupells on Brixton Hill, site adjacent Streatham Hill Congregational Church.

DOUGLAS Louisa, Miss: from 1855 advanced considerable secured loans on Roupell Park to W Roupell.

DOULTON Frederick: son of John, brother to Henry, potters of Lambeth. Friend and supporter of W Roupell, proposed his nomination for MP. Founder member of Volunteers regiment. 1862 succeeded W Roupell as MP.

DOVE Elizabeth: 1871 listed as cook at Aspen House. Widow of Joseph (below)?

DOVE Joseph: land agent at Roupell Park. Witness at 1863 trial.

DUBB: a Roupell employee who witnessed W Roupell's signature.

EDWARDS Thomas: owned and developed land around Upper Tulse Hill adjacent to Roupell Park. 1840-43 a major benefactor of Christ Church.

ELLICE (Ellis) v Roupell: 1862 re Roupell Park deed of gift, deferred for trial outcome.

FORD & LLOYD: solicitors for Waite, 1862 trial.

GABRIEL Messrs: timber merchants, Belvedere Road, Lambeth, supplied Roupell Park 1856.

HASLAM & REES: solicitors, Copthall Court. W Roupell was articled to Haslam 1849-54. Rees acted as WR's solicitor.

HASLAM Mary: widow (of above?) of Roupell Park. 1857 with Emma Roupell at her death in Hastings.

HAWS Daniel: tenant of Bury House, part of Great Warley estate. Witness at 1863 trial. Later tenant of whole estate.

HEWITT WH: receiver.

HUNNUM Mrs: RP Roupell's housekeeper in Cross Street.

HUNTLEY Lord Mr: Roupell's local doctor who delivered R Roupell at Aspen House. Witness at 1862 trial.

LINKLATER James Harvie (Harvey): City solicitor, of J and JH Linklater & Hackwood. 1850 leased Boylands Oak, adjacent to Aspen House. From 1862 acted for R Roupell in trials and other land disputes. He and his wife Isobel were R Roupell's main beneficiaries.

MUGGERIDGE John: of Kennington Cross, business associate and rent collector for RP Roupell. Owned several houses on Roupell Park. Witnessed the forged will.

MUGGERIDGE Henry: son of John. Witness, as were his mother and son, at 1863 trial. Later surveyor of St George's Place, Brixton. Executor to Sarah Roupell's (mother) will.

NICHOL Rev CS: from 1891 vicar at Christ Church. Supported W Roupell. Conducted his funeral service.

OSBORNE Ann: née Brand, of Writtle, Essex, owner of a large estate. Aunt of Catherine Roupell, née Brand, to whom she left a bequest in 1791.

OSBOURNE David: RP Roupell's bailiff. 1841 recorded living at Roupell's cottage, Brixton Hill, with wife and five labourers. 1855 he verified a plan of the 1838 Roupell Park estate.

ORD: surgeon, present at the reading of RP Roupell's will.

POWELL Samuel Goodyear and son William Samuel, law stationers of Parliament Street, who copied deeds for W Roupell. Witnesses at 1862 trial.

RAVEN Rev WODEHOUSE: listed 1851 vicar of Christ Church. 1876 welcomed back W Roupell to Roupell Park on his release.

RING Messrs: of Doctors' Commons, later of Gravesend, RP Roupell's lawyers who drew up his various wills. Witness at 1863 trial.

RHODES: hop merchant of Brixton Road, an instigator of the petition against W Roupell's election campaign who subsequently offered him a bribe.

SHEE Mr Serjeant: senior counsel for R Roupell 1862 and 1863 trials, with Lush QC, Browne and (1863) Thesiger.

SNELL G Blagrave: shorthand writer of the Court of Bankruptcy at 1862 trial.

SPRINGHAM: tenant of Bolens Farm, Great Warley. Witness at 1863 trial.

STEPHENS Richard: of Tulse Hill, one of RP Roupell's executors and trustees.

SURRIDGE James: tenant of Boylands Oak Farm, one of RP Roupell's executors and trustees.

TARTE William: lead merchant of Tothill St. Friend of RP Roupell. Witness at 1862 and 1863 trials.

THOMPSON: clerk at Glyn's Bank and tenant of RP Roupell. Witness at 1863 trial.

THURLOW Lord: Lord Chancellor of England, whose estate, covering much of the present Brixton Hill, Streatham Hill, Tulse Hill and West Norwood in Lambeth, was sold after his death in 1806. The Roupells started purchasing sections in 1810.

TREADWELL John: railway contractor of Leigham Court Estate, adjacent to Roupell Park. 1856 he sold land to RP Roupell via WR who misused the payment cheques. Witness at 1862 trial.

TRUMAN JW: agent for Roupell Park, superintendant of brickfield, founder member and Captain of Volunteers, later publican. Witnessed WR's signature. Witness at 1863 trial.

WAITE JG: 1861 bought Norbiton Park, Kingston, from WR. Defendant in 1862 trial.

WALLET Eleanor: taught W Roupell and siblings in Peckham. 1840 present at R Roupell's birth at Aspen House. Witness at 1862 trial.

WATERLOW: law stationers, copied deeds for W Roupell.

WATKINS: 1862 succeeded Truman as Volunteers' Captain.

WATTS Maria: née Crane. Sister of Sarah Roupell, wife of Walter. Witness at 1862 and 1863 trials.

WATTS Walter: a lawyer. Husband of Maria, W Roupell's uncle. Once articled to attorney King, later Whittaker & King, Grays Inn. By 1853, WR was £1000 in debt to him.

WEBB W: cheesemonger of Blackfriars Road. An executor of John Roupell's will.

WEST James Thomas: Norbiton Park bailiff. Witness at 1862 trial.

WHITTAKER Edward: of Whittaker & King, Grays Inn. From1850 handled W Roupell's affairs including mortgages, starting with Norbiton Farm. Brother Edwin witness at 1863 trial.

WHITTINGTON v Roupell: W Roupell appeared in Roupell Street land dispute 1856.

WILKINSON: 1857 election Liberal candidate (one of three).

WILLIAMS William: 1857 sitting MP for Lambeth. Elected with W Roupell. Founder member of Volunteers regiment.

WOODLEIGH Jane: Sarah Roupell's Pitt Street day servant who continued working at Aspen House. 1840 helped deliver R Roupell. Witness at 1862 and 1863 trials.

WOOD Arthur: gardener, of Lyham Road, Brixton. Witnessed Sarah Roupell's (sister) will. Close friend of William on his release from prison, though much younger. Both worked at Garden Lane nursery.

WOOD Ellen: wife of Arthur (above), later of Harvey Lodge. After his sister's death, looked after W Roupell until his death.

WOODS Sarah Ann: née West, daughter of Norbiton Park bailiff, who kept his accounts. Witness at 1862 trial.

BIBLIOGRAPHY

MAGAZINES and NEWSPAPERS:

The Times: **1820** February 7; **1829** June 1; **1856** December 5; **1857** March 12, 13, 16, 19, 25, 26, 28, 30, 31, August 6; **1858** June 26; **1859** February 2; **1860** January 17; **1861** January 29, 30; **1862** February 4, August 19-23, 26-28, 30, September 8, 16, 20, 24, 25, 26; **1863** January 27, February 17, 28, March 20, April 16, May 8, 9, July 13-28 also as 'The Trial of William Roupell 1863'; **1864** October 4, 6; **1865** February 22, June 12, July 18, December 25; **1869** January 22; **1872** May 8, 10, June 1; **1873** April 16; **1874** October 6; **1876** September 21, 23; **1878** February 4; **1909** March, 27, 30.

Brixton Free Press: **1909** March.

Building News: **1857** August 14.

Fun Magazine

The Globe: **1862** August 26.

Illustrated London News: **1857** April 4, May 9, July 7; **1862** August 23; **1909** March 6.

The Morning Advertiser: **1857** March 16, 24, 25, 31, April 1, July 15, 27.

Punch: **1862** August 30; **1863** August 8.

Roundabout Papers, The: **1860-63** Essays by WM Thackeray published in the Cornhill magazine.

South London News: **1857** July.

South London Press: **1865** January 18; **1878** February 9.

Streatham News: **1909** March 27, April 3; **1916** September 29; **1917** September 21.

BOOKS:

All Change - Kingston, Surbiton & New Malden in the 19th Century *J Sampson*

Annual Register 1862* pages 462-473

Annual Register 1863* pages 264-267

Charlton - A Compilation of the Parish and its People* *JG Smith*

Chronicles of Newgate (published 1884) pages 462-465

Convict Life, by a Ticket-of-Leave Man (published 1880) *Griffiths*

Electoral History of Lambeth, The* (published 1879) pages 129-173 *G Hill*

Great Forgeries of William Roupell, Official Report 1862* (Lambeth Archives)

History of the Parish of Camberwell, The (published 1857) pages 85-89 *WH Blanch*

Lambeth and Southwark Volunteers, The* (published 1955) Chaps 1+ 2 *Tamplin*

Law Report 1862* pages 230-232

Law Report 1863* pages 359-372

Life and Confession of William Roupell* (published 1862) (Harvard Law Library)

Living in Lambeth 1086-1914 pages 49-51 *Nash*

Ramble Round Crystal Palace, A (published 1885) pages 57-58

Rights of Conscience in Danger, The; A letter to William Roupell* (Lambeth Archives)

Story of Norwood, The pages 25 + 26 *JB Wilson*

Surrey Archaeological Collections Volume 2 (1859) page xxvii

Trial of William Roupell, The 1863* (from *The Times*) (Lambeth Archives)

Young Man Said, The - Memoirs of Dennis Wheatley pages 31, 47 *Wheatley*

* Particularly useful

INDEX

Pullman Court, *see St Anne's Society*
Pump Court, Middle Temple 22

Raven Rev Wodehouse 50, 105, 126
Rees see Haslam & Rees
Richard St *see Whittlesey St*
Ring Messrs 66, 68, 71, 72, 74, 94, 126
Rhodes, Mr 48, 126
Roupell family:
Roupell Anne 8, 15, 113
Roupell Catherine 7, 8, 20, 23, 24, 26, 27, 29, 30, 108, 115, 116, 124
Roupell Conrad 7, 8, 13, 14, 113
Roupell Dinah 7, 8, 13-18, 113, 114
Roupell Eleanor Browne 8, 22
Roupell Elizabeth Prioleau 8, 21
Roupell Emma 7, 8, 29, 30, 36, 51, 52, 116-118
Roupell Frances Browne McCulloch 8
Roupell Francis Pooley 8
Roupell George 8, 21
Roupell George Boone 8, 21, 22, 26, 31
Roupell George Leith 8
Roupell John (1695-1759) 7, 8, 14, 18, 19, 113, 114
Roupell John (1733-1777) 7, 8, 15, 18, 19, 114
Roupell John (1761-1835) 7, 8, 19, 20, 22-29, 114-116,
Roupell John (1826-1861) 7, 8, 20, 29, 30, 32, 33, 36, 42, 60, 71, 74, 116, 117, 119
Roupell John Stuart 8
Roupell Mary 7-9, 114, 115
Roupell Patience 7, 8, 15, 18, 19, 114
Roupell Richard 7, 8, 32, 35, 36, 39, 55, 58, 61, 62-80, 87-100, 101, 103-107, 117, 119, 120
Roupell Richard Palmer 7, 8, 20, 23-40, 42, 66-78, 87-100, 115-118
Roupell Robert Prioleau 8
Roupell Sarah 7, 8, 29, 30, 32-34, 36, 39, 42, 59, 61, 67, 68, 70, 77, 96, 101, 103-105, 116-118, 120
Roupell Sarah (1833-1894) 7, 8, 30, 32, 36, 55, 89, 91, 95, 96, 98-108, 116, 117, 120
Roupell Thomas Boone 8

Union Chapel *see Steatham Hill Congregational Church*
Unity Fire Assurance Co 37, 66, 72, 74, 92
Upper Tulse Hill 30, 34

Waite, JG 60, 63-80, 119, 127, *also Norbiton Park*
Wallet, Eleanor 29, 32, 34, 69, 127
Walworth Literary Institution 53
Wandsworth Rd estate 28, 40, 59, 74, 94, 103, 104, 112, 115, 116, 119, 120, 122
Waterlow 91, 127
Watkins 61, 127
Watts, Maria 29, 33, 36, 66, 70, 76, 77, 89, 90, 127
Watts, Walter 33, 36, 66, 68, 70, 72, 77, 80, 88, 90, 91, 97, 99, 117, 127
Webb, W 30, 127
West Norwood 27
West Norwood Cemetery 33, 40, 60, 110, 112, 118, 120
West, James Thomas 66, 69, 127
Wheatley, Dennis 105
Whitehouse Farm, Hants, *see Trunk Farm estate*
Whittaker & King 36, 37, 55, 67, 71, 72, 75, 88, 89, 91, 94, 97-99, 128
Whittington v Roupell 64, 76, 128
Whittlesey St 27, 36, 121
Wilcox Rd *see Wandsworth Rd estate*
Wilkinson 43, 45-47, 49, 128
William of Orange 13, 21, 113
Williams, William 43, 45, 47, 50, 52, 54, 55, 58, 128
Woodleigh, Jane 32, 34, 71, 90, 128
Wood, Arthur & Ellen 108, 109, 128
Woods, Sarah Ann 69, 128
Writtle, nr Chelmsford 24

PRESS REPORTS
AND OTHER PUBLISHED REFERENCES

AUTHOR PROFILE

Judy Harris was born in London in 1944 but spent most of her childhood living in Nunthorpe, then a small village in North Yorkshire, near Middlesbrough. She was educated at Nunthorpe CE Primary School, Middlesbrough High School and Avery Hill College, Eltham, London SE9. From 1965-97, she taught at Fenstanton Junior School, London SW2.

Her interest in local studies began at college with a project on the industrial and residential development of Middlesbrough. Her research into the area around Fenstanton School started in the mid-1970s. However it was not until 1983 that research into the related topics of Roupell Park, the Roupell family and Donald McGill's comic postcards began.

Judy lives in West Norwood and is an active member of the Streatham Society Local History Group and the Southwark & Lambeth Archaeological Society. She produces articles and booklets and gives occasional lectures on her various local history interests.

The Roupells of Lambeth is the culmination of years of somewhat sporadic research. However there are several strands of this complicated but fascinating history which need further attention. It is hoped that the detail presented in this publication will encourage others to fill in the gaps.